A Family Program for Reading Aloud

Second Edition

Part I & Part II

Developed by Rosalie June Slater

FOUNDATION FOR AMERICAN CHRISTIAN EDUCATION
P.O. BOX 27035, SAN FRANCISCO, CALIFORNIA 94127

FOUNDATION FOR AMERICAN CHRISTIAN EDUCATION PUBLICATIONS

The Christian History of the Constitution of the United States of America:
Volume I – *Christian Self-Government*
Volume II – *Christian Self-Government with Union*
The Christian History of the American Revolution: Consider and Ponder
compiled by Verna M. Hall

Teaching and Learning America's Christian History: The Principle Approach
A Family Program for Reading Aloud, Second Edition
by Rosalie J. Slater

Rudiments of America's Christian History and Government: A Student Handbook
The Bible and the Constitution of the United States of America
by Verna M. Hall and Rosalie J. Slater

The American Dictionary of the English Language, Facsimile 1828 Edition
The Value of the Bible and Excellence of the Christian Religion,
for the Use of Families and Schools (1834)
by Noah Webster

The Journal of the Foundation for American Christian Education, featuring
"Partners of a Glorious Hope: Biography of Verna Hall," Vol. I
"The Christian Idea of the Child," Vol. II
"The Revelance of America's Christian History," Vol. III
"The Christopher Columbus Quincentenary," Vol. IV
"Designing a Curriculum for a Christian Civilization," Vol. V, & Vol. VI

Free Publications Catalogue, featuring
THE NOAH PLAN:
A Complete Educational Program in the Principle Approach

COVER PAINTING FROM
JESSIE WILLCOX SMITH: AMERICAN ILLUSTRATOR BY EDWARD NUDELMAN
© 1990 BY EDWARD NUDELMAN
USED BY PERMISSION OF THE PUBLISHER
PELICAN PUBLISHING COMPANY, INC.

A FAMILY PROGRAM FOR READING ALOUD, 2ND EDITION
BY ROSALIE J. SLATER

COPYRIGHT MAY 1, 1991
ISBN 0-912498-09-9
LIBRARY OF CONGRESS CATALOG CARD NUMBER 91-071668

SECOND PRINTING, MAY 1997

DESIGNED BY DESTA GARRETT

PUBLISHED BY
FOUNDATION FOR AMERICAN CHRISTIAN EDUCATION
P.O. BOX 27035, SAN FRANCISCO, CALIFORNIA 94127

Publisher's Preface

A Family Program for Reading Aloud was first published in 1967 and revised in 1983. This **Second Edition** has been expanded by the addition of **Part II**, a previously unpublished study on reading selected authors and subjects "in depth." **Part I** has been edited and the information on the availability and source of the books described has been updated.

In *Reading Aloud,* **Second Edition,** all of the books described have been indexed in the back by author and title, and a list of the publishers with address and/or toll-free phone number for ordering has been provided, as far as this information is available. Books available through F.A.C.E. are marked with an asterisk in the text, and with a double asterisk to indicate that a *Teaching Syllabus* by Rosalie Slater is available with that book.

Many books discussed in **Reading Aloud** are not presently in print. Those known to be out-of-print are marked with the abbreviation "[OP]". You may be able to find them in libraries or used book stores; and they may become available by reprint or republishing in the future. You may check the "Books in Print" in your library or through your local bookseller for current availability.

TABLE OF CONTENTS

Page

PART I HOME LEADERSHIP IN SHAPING CHARACTER THROUGH LITERATURE

INTRODUCTION

    Purposes for a Family Program for Reading Aloud   1

    The Importance of Reading Aloud in Your Home   1

    Skills Needed in Reading Aloud   5

BOOKS TO READ TO YOUNGER CHILDREN

    Mother Goose   7

    Poetry in Your Home   9

    Types of Picture Books and Stories   10

INTRODUCING AMERICA IN YOUR READING ALOUD

    Family Sentiment   14

    The Unity and Diversity of America   17

    Author Study: Marguerite Henry   18

    Learning to Teach the *Principle Approach* with Illustrated Biographies by Ingri and Edgar Parin d'Aulaire   25

    The American Indian in Our Literature   37

    Literature of the Bible Lands   48

EVALUATING YOUR FAMILY READING ALOUD

    Restoring Home as the Educational Center   53

    A Family Accounting of Reading Aloud   60

PART II EXPANDING YOUR INTERESTS THROUGH READING IN DEPTH

INTRODUCTION

      Expanding and Deepening Our Interests Through Reading   61

READING IN DEPTH

    READING ON THE SUBJECT OF THE OCEAN   62

    READING ABOUT THE PIONEERS   64

    READING ABOUT TEACHING AND LEARNING   65

    READING ABOUT THE FRENCH REVOLUTION   66

    READING SOME OF OUR AUTHORS IN DEPTH:

        Charles Dickens   68

        Sir Walter Scott   70

        Washington Irving   72

        Nathaniel Hawthorne   75

RESTORING HEROES AND HEROINES TO OUR READING ALOUD   77

    HEROES

        Hero of Antartica: Admiral Richard E. Byrd   78

        Hero of Modern Aviation: Charles A. Lindbergh   80

        Hero of Wheels and Wings: Eddy Rickenbacker   84

    HEROINES IN OUR HISTORY   90

        Puritan Wife, Mother, Poetess: Anne Bradstreet   91

        Lydia Darrah and Others   95

        Domestic Heroine: Mercy Otis Warren   97

            Chart: *Chain of Christianity*   102

PRESERVERS OF OUR HISTORY

    Ann Pamela Cunningham and the Mount Vernon Ladies' Association   105

    The Charter Oak   114

INDEXES: BOOKS BY TITLE & AUTHOR, AND PUBLISHERS' ADDRESSES   115

PART I

HOME LEADERSHIP IN SHAPING CHARACTER THROUGH LITERATURE

INTRODUCTION

PURPOSES FOR A FAMILY PROGRAM FOR READING ALOUD

American Christian homes have generally relinquished their educational leadership. It was the Christian Home in America which built our nation. Parents formed the character of our American Christian Constitution by first forming the character of their own children. They taught by example and by "precept upon precept."

If we are to restore the vitality of our blessings of liberty under our representative republic we must begin with the revival of the American Christian Home. Parents not educated to *lead* but to *follow,* must once again accept their ability to become Bible students, reasoning from the Word of God, and endeavoring to walk in the ways of the Lord. Then they can direct their children with confidence.

Home is the educational center of our nation. Home education begins with a determination to know and live according to Biblical principles. But it must also include the application of Biblical principles to all fields of learning. Literature is an important field for it deals with "internal" feelings and character. Literature supplies parents and teachers with one of their most useful and beloved avenues of teaching and learning. Literature is the Handmaid of history. It strengthens the study of America's Christian History — Providential History — the Hand of God in all History.

Through the introduction to literature in the Reading Aloud Program families can begin to help shape the *character for liberty* which must be restored to our nation. Just as a nation cannot exist "half slave and half free," so a world cannot exist — with thousands perishing each year under tyranny while we continue to enjoy the blessings of liberty.

"Stand fast therefore in the liberty wherewith Christ hath made us free, and be not entangled with the yoke of bondage." (Galatians 5:1)*

THE IMPORTANCE OF READING ALOUD IN YOUR HOME

God's first institution for society is the home. The home forms the character of the nation. We know that the character of our Founding generations was formed in the Christian homes of America. To restore that character to its full *productive capacity* we need to first restore the home to its educational goal in our republic.

Home is the first sphere of government in our society. "The principle of home-government is love, — love ruling and obeying according to law." As Pastor Phillips stated some one hundred years ago:

---
*All scripture references are to the King James Version.

> The Christian home has its influence also upon the state. It forms the citizen, lays the foundation for civil and political character, prepares the social element and taste, and determines our national prosperity or adversity.[1]

Every area of our society is affected by what the home builds or does not build in character.

If American Christians expect to restore the Biblical principles of government which established our nation, these principles must first be restored in our homes. Home is the first area of local self-government — and it is demonstrated in the lives of all family members.

Literature is one of the tools of learning which can help parents and teachers to get at the *soil* in which Christian character is planted. The heart is the seat of character: "the seat of the affections and passions, as of love, joy, grief, enmity, courage, pleasure, etc." (Noah Webster, *American Dictionary of the English Language,* 1828, F.A.C.E.)

Our Lord spoke of the heart as the source of good and evil: *"A good man out of the good treasure of his heart bringeth forth that which is good; and an evil man out of the evil treasure of his heart bringeth forth that which is evil: for of the abundance of the heart his mouth speaketh."* (Luke 6:45)

Literature deals with *ideals,* with *principles* and with *purposes*. In order to begin the reconstruction of our American Christian character we need to study both the history and literature which identifies our nation. Home is the perfect educational center in which to learn the following:

Who we are as a nation

Where our principles and ideals come from — their sources

What our purpose is as a nation

Establishing the Family Reading Circle is not just a time for each member of the family to be *reading independently.* It is a time for *reading together.* It is a time for *parents* to read aloud those *wise* and *wonderful* books which helped form the character and ideals of America.

The Family Reading Aloud can be one of the most satisfying of family times. But like family Bible Study, it has to be planned and it has to be reserved by every member of the family. Then it will be a time to be cherished and remembered, and best of all, to be perpetuated by your children to the next generation.

A Father Reads to His Family

When Lew Wallace left home as a young man he felt a keen sense of loss, loss of the family readings which had helped shape his mind and heart since his earliest years.

> At home his father's family readings dropped more seed in his son's creative soil than had all the floggings by schoolmasters. These readings and access to his father's library implanted the love of literature in the future novelist. David Wallace bought the best editions of the best books and subscribed to the *Edinburgh Review* and other major British quarterlies. Of contemporary writers, he particularly admired Macaulay, but other favorites included Lamb's *Essays of Elia,* Shakespeare, Milton, and Sir Walter Scott.

---

[1] Phillips, Reverend S., "The Christian Home...," *Teaching and Learning America's Christian History: The Principle Approach,* by Rosalie J. Slater, F.A.C.E., San Francisco (1965), p. 11

> Summer readings were special treats, but on winter nights, the family regularly gathered around the hearth fire and forgot the freezing weather outside, as David Wallace, in a sensitive, well-modulated voice, free from the affectations of professional recitationists, read the histories of Thucydides and Bancroft, the sermons of Chalmers, Hall, Bossuet, and Bourdaloue, and the English poets, essayists, and novelists.[2]

Who could have known that young Lew would become a General in the Union Army, a Governor of New Mexico, and the American minister to Turkey. But most important of all, Lew Wallace was to write the greatest Christian novel of New Testament life, *Ben Hur: A Tale of the Christ*. For more than one hundred years the world has felt closer to the life and times of Jesus Christ by this stirring novel.

Lew Wallace himself was pleased with another aspect of his home training — his father's careful attention to teaching his son detail and accuracy. Years later he was able to verify this in a most exciting discovery:

> Travelers to the Middle East had been struck with the remarkably realistic settings and atmosphere of *Ben Hur,* written at a time when its author had not been out of America. Now Wallace himself was gratified to find how accurate he had been. "I went down into the old Valley of Kedron and from the old well of Enrogel looked over the valley, and every feature of the scene appeared identical with the description of that which the hero of the story looked upon. At every point of the journey over which I traced his steps to Jerusalem, I found the descriptive details true to the existing objects and scenes, and I find no reason for making a single change in the text of the book." He had not only been thorough in his research but had identified with the scenes of his drama by a leap of the artistic imagination.[3]

A Mother Reads to Her Family

Sometimes Mothers are the most frequent Readers Aloud in a family circle. Nora Archibald Smith, writer and sister of Kate Douglas Wiggin, wrote about their mother:

> One of my mother's gifts was that of reading aloud with great charm and expression, and though one of the most reserved persons I ever knew, and one of the most averse to betraying emotion of any kind, she yet lost herself completely at such times and, while her eyes were on the page, would change her voice to suit the various characters in the story, and glow with enthusiasm at their exploits, or quiver with delight. I can see my beloved stepfather, tired with a country doctor's long day, sitting by the winter fire hearing my mother read aloud one of Dicken's novels, which must have been coming out about that time in the paper-covered *Plum Pudding Edition*. We two young things, the little brother being safely tucked away in bed, would be quietly playing in the bay window, perhaps with its stand of English ivy, but we were listening with all our ears nevertheless, to the entrancing tale as it flowed from mother's lips.[4]

---

[2] Morseberger, Robert E. and Katherine M. Morseberger, *Lew Wallace: Militant Romantic*, McGraw-Hill Book Company, New York (1980), p. 17
[3] *Ibid.*, p. 334
[4] Smith, Nora Archibald, *Kate Douglas Wiggin, As Her Sister Knew Her*, Houghton Mifflin Company, Boston (1925), p. 9

The culmination of the home reading for Kate Douglas Wiggin was *A Child's Journey with Dickens* in which she described her train ride with the great author. Discovering that he was on the same train she dared to sit down beside him and discuss his novels with all the candor of an adult critic — yet with the spontaneity of a child. As Mrs. Wiggin concluded from her own childhood experience with literature:

CHARLES DICKENS

> It seems to me that no child nowadays has time to love an author as the children and young people of that generation loved Dickens; nor do I think that any living author of today provokes love in exactly the same fashion. From our yellow dog, Pip, to the cat, the canary, the lamb, the cow, down to all the hens and cocks, almost every living thing was named, sooner or later, after one of Dicken's characters; while my favorite sled, painted in brown, with the title in brilliant red letters, was *The Artful Dodger*.[5]

Kate Douglas Wiggin became a popular author herself writing some unforgettable juveniles, *The Bird's Christmas Carol, Mother Carey's Chickens,* and her best known *Rebecca of Sunnybrook Farm* which was widely dramatized on stage and screen.

Horace Elisha Scudder, 1838–1902, editor and author, wrote:

> Above all there is great virtue in reading to the young, rather than leaving them to silent reading. We are getting into a sort of sociability which consists in a household sitting in the evening round a table, very likely with backs all to the light, for the sake of saving weak eyes, each reading to himself, —
>
> *All silent, and all —*
>
> Of all people, children should be spared this refinement of civilization. If we would only consider the subtle strengthening of ties which comes from two people reading the same book together, breathing at once its breath and each giving the other unconsciously his interpretation of it, it would be seen how, in this simple habit of reading aloud, lies a power too fine to analyze, yet stronger than iron in welding souls together. To our thinking, there is no academy on earth equal to that found in so many homes, of a mother reading to her child.[6]

Parents Let Go of Home Education

American Christian parents began to lose control over their children when they relinquished home Reading Aloud. As they turned over the education of their children to outside agencies, even to the Sunday School and to the Christian School, they lost a critical part of their intimate relationship with their children. Many wonderful teachers have gained by what parents let go — yet parents alone have opportunities which are never afforded to those outside the realm of home.

---

[5] Wiggin, Kate Douglas, *A Child's Journey with Dickens,* from the *Writings of Kate Douglas Wiggin,* (Autograph Edition, Volume One), Houghton Mifflin Company, Boston (1917), p. 295

[6] Schudder, Horace Elisha, Editor, *The Riverside Magazine for Young People,* Volume 1, Hurd and Houghton, New York (1867), p. 45

A major purpose of the Christian History Literature Program is to help you recapture your family opportunities for learning. The Reading Aloud Program can help you first "catch up on the classics," on those books of substance, character, and interest, which require careful teaching to the young. As you are introduced to authors who have made a contribution to literature on the Chain of Christianity perhaps you, too, will come to love some of those men and women whose ideals, principles, and literary talents have not yet blessed and enriched the present generation of young people. With your inspiration and Reading Aloud these wonderful treasures can be perpetuated to the next generation.

The Bible admonishes often to *hold fast that which is good.* And since the *government, education,* and *character* which comes out of the American Christian Home also constitutes the *government, education,* and *character of the nation,* we need to:

Stand fast therefore in the liberty wherewith Christ hath made us free, and be not entangled again with the yoke of bondage. (Galatians 5:1)

SKILLS NEEDED IN READING ALOUD

Noah Webster in his *Introduction to the Origin of Language* in the 1828 *American Dictionary of the English Language* states:

It is therefore probable that *language* as well as the faculty of speech, was the *immediate gift of God.*

This gift includes the *Voice,* source of sound, *Tone,* or accent and inflection of the voice, and *Expression,* that which identifies the ideas, convictions, and feelings of the speaker. These three elements are both internal and external. They make the difference between Reading Aloud that is monotonous and difficult to listen to, and that which is modulated. Modulation refers to "the act of inflecting the voice in reading or speaking; a rising or falling of the voice." This becomes the instrument of the Reader. If you love what you are reading; if you are interested in arousing the feelings of your listeners; if you know the message of the author and you wish to help convey it; all of these aspects will help you to use your voice effectively.

It is important for the Reader Aloud to know the author and the book so that he or she brings to it a "preparation" of the heart so that *"the answer of the tongue is from God."* (Proverbs 16:1) Fine literature affords so many avenues for teaching the Truths of God that we need to carefully take advantage of opportunities with our children or our students so that we may enrich their minds, and hearts and character.

Learning to Listen

Noah Webster, in his 1828 *American Dictionary,* defines *Listening* in part as "To hearken, to give ear; to attend closely with a view to hear."

Listening Skills have to be cultivated and learned. This becomes of mutual concern to both the Reader and the Listener. The Reader should watch his or her audience. Look up often. Keep eye and mind contact. This helps the Listener who must become convinced that the Reader has something important to communicate. As Horace Scudder writes, Reading Aloud is "stronger than iron in welding souls together." Once you discover the satisfaction of reading aloud a book to your family or class, you will find that it has bound you closer to your listeners, to a unity of ideals and character.

But Listening is a skill which in this day and age is most difficult to attain. Many different sounds are bombarding us constantly. Also, many individuals do not have that internal peace and contentment which help them "turn off" the competing sounds and enable them to concentrate on the reading aloud. To concentrate requires mental effort — a "centering" of thoughts around a focus or target. If the Listener allows thought to wander off from the point of the reading — the impact of the book will be lost. Both Reader and Listener will be disappointed. Paying attention requires both a mental and an emotional effort.

Reading Aloud can be cultivated with both Reader and Listeners by gradually increasing the length of reading time and watching for signs of fatigue and disinterest. It is amazing how much you can read and how often you can Read Aloud when you have built up the interest in a book in which you believe. Persist wisely and help your Listeners past the first difficulties of a new author until you have reached "smooth sailing" and they are with you emotionally and intellectually.

Reading Aloud is most helpful in cultivating mental skills. Review at each reading what has gone before in plot, character development, and setting. Cultivate the imagination of your Listeners and allow them to discuss what they think will result from certain aspects of character, certain directions of the plot. We need to develop the ability to use our minds when we are not encumbered with note-taking, or book reports, etc.

Reading Aloud is a mental trip through an author's mind. We come to know how the author feels through the characters; how he or she reasons through the plot; how the use of words can create for us descriptive images of people, places, and things we never had thought of before. Literature allows us to experience many things through the development of the imagination. It allows us to go to many places where we might never go. It expands the horizons of mind and heart. It increases our awareness of time — past, present, and future.

How well is your "house" — your mind — furnished? Do you, like Louisa May Alcott, "enjoy your mind?" Literature helps to furnish our mental homes with permanent fixtures, with "all things wise and wonderful," with Scriptural objects of beauty — the result of reflection. The American Prisoners of War who had committed much to their minds of literature, of poetry learned by heart, of Bible memory, were better able to endure the external conditions of their imprisonment. What have we in the house? Does it enrich ourselves and others?

BOOKS TO READ TO YOUNGER CHILDREN

MOTHER GOOSE

> The rhymes of Mother Goose free the fancy, charm the tongue and ear, delight the inward eye, and many of them are tiny masterpieces of word craftsmanship. (Walter de la Mare)

Children love the Mother Goose Rhymes because:

1) The subject matter is interesting to them
2) They are rhythmical — with a regular accent and beat
3) They are full of humor of the non-sense variety

And Mother Goose is part of our English Heritage. These delightful verses are humorous portraits of historic personages, of places, or of events. *Little Jack Horner* really did "pull out a plum" from the pie he was carrying. It was a title deed to one of the church estates which *Henry the VIII* was repossessing. Jack was rewarded and his "plum" became "the house that Jack built."

The Nursery Rhyme that begins "Sing a song of sixpence" and includes scenes of the "king in his counting house, counting out his money, and the queen was in the parlor eating bread and honey" are supposed to refer to *Henry the VIII* and *Katherine of Aragon* eating the bread of England coated with the honey of Spain's assurances that she will not be divorced by Henry. But "the maid in the garden, hanging out the clothes" is *Anne Boleyn,* whose new wardrobe from France will clothe her for a thousand days before her fate is sealed by the executioner's axe. "Along came a blackbird and snipped off her nose."

And *Little Miss Muffet* is reputed to be *Mary Queen of Scots*. The "big black spider" who "sat down beside her" is John Knox, Scottish reformer who is denouncing her frivolous ways.

What fun when you and your children make the transition from these Nursery jingles that ripple off the tongue, to discover English History. When you visit England you may not find that "London Bridge" can fall down into the Thames River. It is no longer in England but in Arizona. But you may still "Ride a cock-horse to Banbury Cross" — now Charing Cross and take tea and recite the old rhyme with pleasure.

Here are some recommended books for you so that you can teach and learn those Nursery Rhymes which introduce your family to the basic rhythm patterns of the English Language and which are also delightful excursions into the realm of the imagination.

Book of Nursery and Mother Goose Rhymes by Marguerite de Angeli (1954), from Bantam Doubleday Dell.* This is the most charming of many Mother Goose books and both cloth and paperback editions are available.

---

*Books marked with an asterisk (*) can be ordered from F.A.C.E.; books marked with a double asterisk (**) also have a *Teaching Syllabus* by Rosalie Slater available. See Indexes in the back of this book for ordering information.

The Annotated Mother Goose by William S. and Ceil Barring-Gould (1962), from Penguin USA. Catch up on the history and the illustrators of Mother Goose.

The Oxford Nursery Rhyme Book by Iona and Peter Opie (1955), Oxford University Press. Here is a wealth of "infant jingles, riddles, catches, tongue-trippers, baby games, toe names, maxims, alphabets, counting rhymes, prayers, and lullabies, with which generation after generation of mothers and nurses have attempted to please the youngest, and have, somehow, usually succeeded." A book to introduce your children to both the oral and written literary heritage of our language.

In *Children and Books,* 3rd Edition (1964), from Scott, Foresman & Co., the author, May Hill Arbuthnot, suggests that "it is a rewarding task to make a list of the different kinds of verses in *Mother Goose.*" How many categories can you identify?

Counting Rhymes: One, two, buckle my shoe; etc.

Alphabets: A was an apple pie; etc.

Superstitions: See a pin and pick it up; etc.

Time Verses: Thirty days hath September; etc.

Days of the Week: Solomon Grundy, born on Monday; etc.

Verse Stories: The Queen of Hearts, she made some tarts; etc.

Dialog: Who killed Cock Robin? etc.

Songs: A frog he would a-wooing go; etc.

Street Cries: Hot-cross buns; etc.

Weather: Rain, rain, go away; etc.

Tongue Twisters: Peter Piper picked a peck of pickled peppers; etc.

Cumulative Stories: This is the house that Jack built; etc.

Nonsense: Three wise men of Gotham; etc.

Select some rhymes for their musical quality. After the children know them by heart they can skip, gallop, run, walk, swing, trot, hop to the sound of them. Mother Goose helps memory, imagination, and speech — for enunciation clear, crisp, and in rhythm brings joy to the listener as well as the performer.

POETRY IN YOUR HOME

Children brought up on the lyrical language and cadence of the King James Bible have laid the first cornerstone for their love and delight in poetry. Nursery Rhymes and Mother Goose ditties also contribute much to the music and sound of words. Poetry can begin early and it should be first a love of the parents — Fathers and Mothers need to recapture their love of and knowledge of poetry.

A Child's Book of Poems, pictures by Gyo Fujikawa (1969), from The Putnam Publishing Group.* This is a book for parents to browse through and reacquaint themselves with many of our outstanding English and American poets. Yet with the profuse illustrations of Gyo Fujikawa the offerings are well balanced and charming in black and white and color. Find the poems that appeal to you and share them with your children; they will respond with what they enjoy. Then begin to memorize and store up your mental home with furnishings you can recall at any moment. Many of the children's poets are actually our famous poets and this particular volume has included a fine representative sampling as an introduction. Note the names and begin to identify their style with the intention of making a fuller investigation of their work.

Robert Louis Stevenson's *A Child's Garden of Verses*, also from Putnam, has been published in a companion edition and illustrated by Gyo Fujikawa.* This is a classic of poetry written by Stevenson looking back fondly upon his childhood and dedicated to his nurse, Alison Cunningham. It reveals the imagination and reasoning of a "reading" and "thinking" mind and contains much treasure to be stored in mind and heart. At the proper time you will want to find a biography of Stevenson to read to your family. One such biography written for children is:

Robert Louis Stevenson: Storyteller and Adventurer by Katharine Wilkie (1961), Piper Book, Houghton Mifflin Co.

Divine Songs in Easy Language for the Use of Children by Isaac Watts (1674–1748), is a book of poetry by a Puritan theologian and hymnist. It was much appreciated during Colonial and Revolutionary years in our country. It went out of print, but photocopies are available from the Cumberland Missionary Society. In these verses the American Christian child is reminded how to put his Christian faith into practice in all daily activities. (See "Correcting the Temper," by James B. Rose, *Journal I*, F.A.C.E.)

The Oxford Book of Children's Verse, chosen and edited by Iona and Peter Opie (1973), Oxford University Press. This is a treasury of British and American classics spanning five hundred years. Its 332 entries were chosen, in the words of the editors, as "verses that have been written for children, or written with children prominently in mind, which either were cherished in their own day, or have stood the test of time." This volume contains some poetry hard to find in other collections, especially some choice poems by William Blake (1757–1827), for example:

The Lamb

Little lamb, who made thee?
Dost thou know who made thee?
Gave thee life, and bid thee feed
By the stream and o'er the mead;
Gave thee clothing of delight,
Softest clothing, woolly, bright;
Gave thee such a tender voice,
Making all the vales rejoice?
Little lamb, who made thee?
Dost thou know who made thee?

Little lamb, I'll tell thee,
Little lamb, I'll tell thee:
He is called by thy name,
For he calls himself a lamb.
He is meek, and he is mild;
He became a little child.
I a child, and thou a lamb,
We are called by his name.
Little lamb, God bless thee!
Little lamb, God bless thee!

The Home Book of Verse for Young Folks, selected and arranged by Burton Egbert Stevenson (1915), Hold, Rinehart and Winston [OP],* is an excellent collection which will carry you to High School. It contains the poems we have all loved and ranges from nursery rhymes to fairyland to patriotism. A basic book to continue our heritage of literature, character, and liberty.

American History in Verse, arranged and edited by Burton Stevenson, republished by Bob Jones University. Mr. Stevenson has done a great service in arranging this collection of our great patriotic poetry chronologically. We can begin with Christopher Columbus — *Sail on! Sail on! Sail on! and on!* We can follow the Pilgrims and travel through all our history including World War I. It is an excellent way to recall and commemorate our dramatic history.

TYPES OF PICTURE BOOKS AND STORIES

Pelle's New Suit by Elsa Beskow, Harper & Row. It is a rare thing to see things "whole" and "complete." Pelle's little lamb gives the wool to start the steps in making a suit for Pelle. This is the story of how Pelle works to help those who are making the suit for him. Finally, on Sunday morning, he has a new blue suit to wear. And the lamb seems pleased, too.

---
*[OP], means currently out-of-print.

The Runaway Bunny by Margaret Wise Brown (1942), pictures by Clement Hurd, Harper & Row Junior Books. "Once there was a little bunny who wanted to run away... but no matter where he went, or how far he tried to go Mother said: 'If you run away, I will run after you. For you are my little bunny.'" Mother's reassuring love finally convinces little bunny. "Shucks, I might just as well stay where I am and be your little bunny." And so he did.

The Little House by Virginia Lee Burton (1942), Houghton Mifflin & Company. The Little House was a strong, well-built house. She lived in the country and enjoyed God's seasons. But the city finally grew up around her and totally obscured her. She had to be rediscovered, for though her outside was "cracked and shabby" — underneath, she was just as good a house as ever. It was the builder's great-great-granddaughter who rescued the Little House and returned her to the country where she could enjoy the seasons and be what she was intended to be.

Maybelle, The Cable Car by Virginia Lee Burton (1952), Houghton Mifflin & Company [OP]. Maybelle, the Cable Car in San Francisco is celebrated in this charming book about the struggle to maintain the individuality of this unique form of transportation so dear to both tourists and citizens of the city.

Mike Mulligan and His Steam Shovel by Virginia Lee Burton (1939), Houghton Mifflin & Company. Mary Anne felt the passage of time as the new, fast, and efficient Diesel motor shovels took over. But when Mike offered to dig free the cellar for the new town hall of Popperville, he did not realize he was digging a future for both him and his faithful Mary Anne.

The Story About Ping by Marjorie Flack and Kurt Wiese (1933), Puffin Picture Book, Penguin USA. Eleven ducks have individuality and this little Chinese duck, living with his family on the Yangtze River has to learn that it is better to be spanked and be at home than suffer the dangers of a world that might devour him.

Millions of Cats by Wanda Gag (1939), The Putnam Publishing Group (Coward). This is a wonderful book to read and recite. "Hundreds of cats, thousands of cats, millions and billions and trillions of cats." But there is always only one — just for you, "The most beautiful cat in the world."

The Gingerbread Boy by Paul Galdone (1975), Houghton Mifflin & Company. Paul Galdone takes the old folk tale and with text and large friendly illustrations he provides us with another treatment of the old story. "Run, run, run. Catch me if you can. You can't catch me. I am the Gingerbread Boy, I am, I am." But he was outfoxed and went the way of all Gingerbread boys.

Little Toot by Hardie Gramatky (1939), The Putnam Publishing Group. Little Toot the Tugboat had not learned to be self-governed. He was, in fact, totally irresponsible. But when a desperate situation arose requiring some thinking and action, Little Toot proved himself. He changed his character and became helpful and loved.

The Big Snow by Berta and Elmer Hader (1948), Macmillan Publishing Co., Caldecott Award, [OP]. "There is a time for everything." Seasons have signs and these are part of God's rhythmic round of the continuity of life. For every season there is a preparation as in this season before the Big Snow. How do God's creatures prepare for an especially cold winter season?

Make Way for the Ducklings by Robert McCloskey (1941), Caldecott Award, Puffin Picture Book, Penguin USA. Mr. and Mrs. Mallard hatched their ducklings on an island in the Charles River. The city hazards began when Mrs. Mallard marched her ducklings to meet Father Mallard in the Boston Public Gardens. (Brown and white illustrations)

Time of Wonder by Robert McCloskey (1957), Caldecott Award. In beautiful watercolor, Mr. McCloskey identifies the uniqueness and individuality of a Maine island. His prose is as lovely as his illustrations and we enjoy the beauty of a Maine morning and watch what happens when a hurricane is announced, when it comes, and afterwards. A truly artistic and poetic book.

The Little Engine That Could by Watty Piper (1941), The Putnam Publishing Group (G & D). Only the Little Blue Engine was concerned and willing to try and help pull the train over the mountain. "I am not very big, but, I think I can, I think I can." Was she successful?

The Tale of Peter Rabbit and other stories by Beatrix Potter (1901), F. Warne & Company, Penguin USA. The consummate artistry of Beatrix Potter developed through her careful and loving interest in the natural world of her childhood and her efforts to draw what she observed. She is a master of detail with an economy of line. Her color compliments her excellent phrasing of the English language. Simple sentences, well controlled like the English, like her brush, enable her to convey the essence of her story line.

> Beatrix Potter ultimately wrote and illustrated 23 books in all... her love for nature, nurtured in her early years, instilled in Beatrix a great need to preserve the English Lake District... to pet her animals — her best and only childhood friends and the "stars" of her beloved stories — she gave human qualities for she knew them so well, their habits and characteristics. Her special understanding of them and her deep appreciation and respect for nature herself is the magic ingredient in Beatrix Potter's work. (1977 Castle Books)

The Velveteen Rabbit by Margery Williams, Illus. by William Nicholson (1926), Bantam Doubleday Dell; available in many different editions at your bookstore. Do toys come to life if they are loved enough? That is the theme of this story — and a point you might have wondered about yourself.

Parents! *"Provoke not your children to wrath."*

Where the Wild Things Are by Maurice Sendak (1963), Harper & Row Junior Books. This book received the Caldecott Medal for the "most distinguished picture book of the year." Sendak has been highly successful as a contemporary author with much appeal for children. Why? Perhaps we as parents and teachers can learn something special from this book. It is a book for *us* to read. Perhaps later you can read it to a child who would understand why Christian families have such an important part to play in our nation.

When you first look at this book you will recognize a part of the message as the pictures in their *colors,* their *distortions* and the *juxtaposition of reality* and *unreality* tell us of the feelings of the small boy "Max." Max is angry and frustrated and he seeks to take out his anger on everything around him. Finally, Mother becomes frustrated, and Mother classifies him as a "wild thing." Mother is not visible — but she is heard offstage. She is not near him, but she banishes him to bed without anything to eat — without "nurture."

Max's revenge is to fantasize his escape to "the wild things." When he arrives at "the place where the wild things are" he takes "dominion over them" — he becomes their king. It is he who decrees that these ferocious *distortions* of God's Creatures shall indulge in a "wild rumpus" and so they do. It is a wild melee in which Max joins until even he tires of the orgy and sends "the wild things off to bed without their supper." He is lonely — and wants to be "where someone loved him best of all." He could even "smell" "good things to eat" — nurture.

Max leaves his "wild things" — despite their protestations of love for him. And when he arrives home "into the night of his very own room" he finds "his supper waiting for him — and it was still hot."

Our hearts yearn for the Maxes of the world who feel "wild things" in their hearts yet do not have the kind of parents who will take their children into their arms and teach them how to deal with life and its frustrations. Perhaps the author intended to celebrate the world of many small boys and girls — whose parents are too busy to help them deal with their emotions and dispositions. All too often they are banished further from the land of the loving. In this book the most poignant picture is the last — where Max finds his supper — and *there is no one there — no parent to greet him back.*

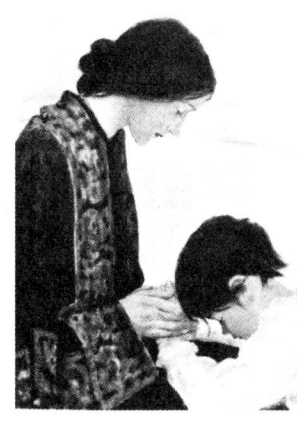
by Jessie Willcox Smith

We wonder what will happen when the Maxes of this country grow up. How will they deal with their frustrations? Will they have to go to "the place where the wild things are" or will some farseeing parent have prepared the way to Christian self-government and obedience to the Lord, so that the "rod" of dominion over Satan will prevail? We need parents who will bring their children up *"in the nurture and admonition of the Lord"* and will not further *"provoke them to wrath."* Read Ephesians Chapter Six.

Let's keep the "wild things" *internal* and deal with them there. Let us not relegate our children to an *external* place where the "wild things" live.

INTRODUCING AMERICA IN YOUR READING ALOUD

FAMILY SENTIMENT

Perhaps the biggest change in American Literature today — in both juvenile and adult literature — is the change in how family life is portrayed. Nor is family life a central theme in today's literature. We have to go back to an earlier day when parents and children openly expressed their affection for each other. Some of our most famous books of the nineteenth century and early twentieth century celebrated family life. These books, for the most part, can be found in your local library — or old bookstore.

Five Little Peppers and How They Grew by Margaret Sidney (1936), The Putnam Publishing Group (G & D). The Pepper family would today be considered far below the poverty level — and they were poor — yet rich in love towards each other. Mrs. Pepper, a widow, struggled to keep the family fed on a meager income and with the older chldren earning a few pennies a week. It was a time when electricity was not available to many homes. Candles cost money — but there was a willingness to work and to help each other and to sacrifice for others. This is a book which should give American children of today pause for consideration as to how much affluence and how many material things they seem to need to be happy.

Mother Carey's Chickens by Kate Douglas Wiggin, Grossett & Dunlap, NY (1911). Republished by the Foundation for American Christian Education in 1991.

Mrs. Carey is widowed at the beginning of the book. This is a most heartwarming book about how a family of four children rally around their Mother to cope with their new situation. While Mrs. Pepper and her children lacked education, Mrs. Carey and her family enjoy a background of literature. Their move to a tiny Maine village, and to the Yellow House, which had actually been discovered by their Father on a picnic, is a story of character struggles. Each child has some lessons to learn. Gilbert must

"COME HOME, CHILDREN!"

give up the idea of an expensive and famous college. "You can't have the help of Yale or Harvard or Bowdoin to make a man of you, my son, — you will have to fight your own battles and win your own spurs."

One of the blessings of the Careys' move to Beulah, Maine is their effect upon that small village. Much is given, much exchanged, and the book creates lovely images of family living and learning. Charles Kinglsey's *Water Babies* is the backdrop for this story.

If it fits the tempo of your own heart and mind, you will cherish reading and rereading this delightful book.

The Bird's Christmas Carol by Kate Douglas Wiggin, Bantam Doubleday Dell. Carol Bird was born on Christmas Day. And she went home on that day, too, but not before she had "done what God sent her for." Carol herself put it into these words when speaking to her Uncle Jack:

> Long ago, when I first began to be ill, I used to think, the first thing when I waked up Christmas morning, "Today is Christ's birthday — *and mine!*" I did not put the words close together, you know, because that made it seem too bold; but I first said, "Christ's birthday" out loud, and then, in a minute softly to myself — *"and mine!"* "Christ's birthday — *and mine!*" ...Now, Uncle Jack dear, I am going to try to make somebody happy every single Christmas that I live and this year it is to be the "Ruggleses in the rear."

What a contrast to our treatment of a child terminally ill today. We endeavor to give the child everything it might miss. Instead, this child is allowed to "give" of herself — and this means so much to her and to all of those who are part of her earthly life.

Rebecca of Sunnybrook Farm by Kate Douglas Wiggin, Airmont Publishing Co., Inc.* It is hard to realize that when this book first appeared it was enjoyed by adults as well as by young people. We were still an innocent people before World War I. We were unsophisticated and genuine in our love for Rebecca Rowena (named for the Saxon Princess in *Ivanhoe*) Randall.

Rebecca, a bouncing, vital, and determined little girl, is sent to live with her aunts — away from the family — so that she might enjoy an education. Aunt Mirandy was a pious Christian woman and not responsive to a spirited young lady and so a character struggle and a difference of temperaments ensue. But with the tender mercies of Aunt Jane, Rebecca is able to endure and the result is growth in Christian qualities of character — both for Rebecca and Aunt Mirandy.

Rebecca was welcomed by audiences as it became a play and a motion picture.

Kate Douglas Wiggin, the author of the last three books, was the little girl who traveled on the train with Charles Dickens and visited with him. Her family "reading aloud" and her own reading of Shakespeare and the Bible, prepared her to become both a teacher and a writer. In fact, in 1878 she organized the first free kindergarten on the Pacific coast in San Francisco. Here she found much inspiration for her writing.

The Swiss Family Robinson by J. R. Wyss, (G&D), The Putnam Publishing Group. This has been a favorite family book for more than one hundred years. Written by Johann Wyss (1743–1818), a Swiss Army chaplain, it is the imaginary experience of a family wrecked on an island and building a life for themselves. Naturally there are strange foods and animals and the family utilize their resources to build a house in the tree, and corral animal power and animal food. Today we may sometimes find ourselves a little shocked at the abrupt killing of an animal — although many become pets or are left alone. On the whole it is an ingenious account of survival — and it always appeals to the imagination. What would you do in such a situation?

The family prays together often and endeavors to lead a Christian life.

Little Women by Louisa May Alcott, The Putnam Publishing Group (G&D).** In 1868 a young New England woman wrote what was to become our most famous classic about family living and loving. *Little Women* is a wonderful book for a contemporary family to live with — for it will take a "heap of reading" to finish the more than 600 pages of the March family life. But it is a book which will be of "life-changing" value — if you allow it to become a part of your own family learning. You need to read it for yourself as a parent or a teacher — in order to plan for the events which will come and the feelings which are to be dealt with by the author.

Louisa May Alcott wrote many books — but none which touched the mind and heart as this one, for it was based in part upon her own family. The Alcotts were poor by the world's standards — but rich in learning, in character, in devotion to ideals of life and living. Against the backdrop of the Civil War and with a foreground of John Bunyan's great Christian classic, *Pilgrim's Progress,* the chapters are woven. The Alcott girls — the Little Women — have many male characters to support them. There is Father March, a Chaplain in the War; Grandfather Lawrence, the kindly neighbor; of course, Laurie, the rich young neighbor; and dear John Brooks who is to marry the first Alcott girl, Meg.

This is a book to work towards — for it must really become one of the most important books that you read aloud together, as a family.

Invincible Louisa by Cornelia Meigs, Alcott Centennial Edition. First published in 1933, this biography won the Newbery Medal for that year. It is a delightful portrait of Louisa May Alcott and truly a literary biography for parent, teacher, or student.

The Yearling by Marjorie Kinnan Rawlings, N. C. Wyeth, Illustrator (1938), Scribner Illustrated Classic, decorated by Edward Shenton, from Macmillan Publishing Co. Winner of the 1939 Pulitzer Prize for the best novel written in America, this is the story of a Florida family, the Baxters, and of a boy's friendship with a wild fawn. The struggle in backwoods Florida to survive is complicated by the fawn — and this becomes the classic theme — of a boy becoming a man — and of a family able to survive the boy's greatest trauma and conflict of feeling. It is a not a book for the very young, but for the mature who can relate the book's courage to their own lives. A good book to talk about in the family circle, it will be a book of pure delight — and of tears.

Every book you read in your family should be prepared ahead of reading aloud and should invite interest and study.

THE UNITY AND DIVERSITY OF AMERICA

So America adopts the children of all lands only to return a manhood ennobled by a sense of its own dignity through the practice of a system of self-government which improves the condition and promotes the interest of each while it produces harm to none. (Hall, *Christian History,* VOL. I, p. 8)

America is the only nation made up of all nations and races. Here "the Englishman, the German, the Frenchman, the Italian, the Scandinavian, the Asiatic and the African all meet as equals. [Here] they are free to speak, to think and to act. They bring the common contributions of a character, energy and activity to the support and enlargement of a common country, and the spread of its influence and enlightenment through all the lands of its origin." (Hall, *Christian History,* VOL. I, p. 8)

Phillis Wheatley, America's First Black Poetess by Miriam Morris Fuller (1971), Garrard Pub. Co. This biography is only an introduction. Her poetry must be sought elsewhere. To appreciate Phillis Wheatley one needs to study America's Christian History and Literature.

The Poems of Phillis Wheatley, edited and with an introduction by Julian D. Macon, Jr. (1966), University of North Carolina Press [OP]; other editions are available.

by Victor Mays

Amos Fortune, Free Man by Elizabeth Yates (1950), the Newbery Award, from E. P. Dutton, Div. of Penguin. Born in Africa, like Phillis Wheatley, Amos Fortune was brought to Massachusetts at fifteen in 1710. Here he lived as a slave until, at age sixty, he was able to purchase his freedom. He moved to Jaffrey, New Hampshire where he became an expert tanner and a respected citizen. On his tombstone one can read: "Who was born free in Africa, a slave in America, who purchased his liberty, professed Christianity, lived reputably, and died hopefully."

Leo Politi and our *Mexican-Americans.*

Leo Politi has contributed much to our understanding of the Mexican-Americans in California. He has two charming books entitled *Pedro, the Angel of Olvera Street* and *Juanita,* which are out-of-print. In *Song of the Swallows,* Macmillan Publishing Co., he deals with the Mission of San Juan Capistrano and the annual return of the swallows on St. Joseph's day. In *The Butterflies Come,* [OP], it is the mysterious return of the Monarch Butterflies to the Monterey Peninsula each year.

Margaret de Angeli and the *Unity* and *Diversity* of America

Mrs. de Angeli has written and illustrated a number of books dealing with the unique national and racial groups in our country. Here are some selections which are particularly well done. We remember Mrs. de Angeli as the illustrator of her *Book of Nursery and Mother Goose Rhymes*. These four books are from Doubleday.

Thee Hannah. Quaker bonnets are plain, with no ribbons. How does a little Quaker girl learn that the individuality of her bonnet means something special and important to others?

Henner's Lydia is a little Amish girl who lives on a farm near Lancaster, Pennsylvania. All summer long Lydia struggles to finish her first little hooked mat so that she can go to market with her father. This book is a delightful expression of our Pennsylvania Dutch heritage [OP].

Up the Hill, the story of a Polish girl, Aniela, living in a Pennsylvania mining town, is a lovely tribute to the Polish people who have contributed to the unity and diversity of America [OP].

Bright April is the story of a bright Negro child struggling to be accepted for herself as an American [OP].

A Regional Book

Blue Willow by Doris Gates (1940), A Newbery Honor Book, Puffin Book, Penguin USA. One of the most charming of all our regional books for children, this book deals with the white, itinerant farm workers in the San Joaquin Valley of California. The Blue Willow plate that Janey Larkin keeps as her treasure is the *only symbol of permanence* in a life of change. But the Blue Willow plate and Janey and her family do find a home and permanence as the story unfolds. It is a good book for our *affluent children* to read today — it helps us appreciate what home can mean and should mean to us all.

AUTHOR STUDY: MARGUERITE HENRY

A contemporary American writer for children and young
people of true stories about horses and some key Americans.

Biblically, Mrs. Henry fulfills our Scriptural admonition to teach:

Finally, brethren, whatsoever things are true, whatsoever things are honest, whatsoever things are just, whatsoever things are pure, whatsoever things are lovely, whatsoever things are of good report; if there be any virtue, and if there be any praise, think on these things. (The Apostle Paul, Philippians 4:8)

Historically, Mrs. Henry fulfills our standards for accuracy and emphasis of individual character and productivity and responsibility as the basis of our Republic.

Nathaniel Hawthorne, in his stories for children, upheld a "deep sense of responsibility. He would not for the world cast anything into the fountain of a young heart, that might embitter and pollute its waters."

A survey and study of contemporary children's literature reveals that those secular authorities for reviewing and recommending children's books do not take this standard as their criterion. That is why it is critical for American Christian teachers to have both a philosophy of literature, an understanding of the history of children's literature in this country, and to have developed their own Biblical and historical measure of each author they select for teaching in their school or at home. This also applies to the books which we must help students to select for their outside or recreational reading.

It is therefore most satisfying to find some authors who by their own individual character and lifestyle support the principles which American Christian educators believe are critical for the minds and hearts — the nurture of their students or children. Here is an author you should know better: Mrs. Marguerite Henry.

Marguerite Henry — Authoress Par Excellence

> Coming home from Sunday School one bright morning in April, I found a surprise to set the heart of any five-year-old rejoicing. It was a baby sister, cradled in the elbow of a plump, starched stranger, the long white baby dress flowing into the crisp apron of the nurse. Gazing rapturously, I was assured that she was really mine, and allowed to hold her in my lap for a moment, to inspect the tiny head with its soft brown hair and to feel the tendril fingers close round my stubby thumb. For a long moment my heart overflowed with emotion toward the sleeping infant; then I hastily relinquished her to my brother so that I might dash out of the house to spread the news among all my playmates and neighbors. I have been boasting about that little sister ever since.

This was the splendid introduction by her older sister upon the reception in 1949 by Marguerite Henry of the Newbery Award, presented each year to "the author of the most distinguished contribution to American literature for children." This Award was presented for her book *King of the Wind*. Marguerite and her older sister, Gertrude Jupp, continued to be supportive of each other during the years of writing and research, and we find her name listed in Mrs. Henry's books as one who had helped with the book production.

> Being the youngest in a family of five, with four of them old enough to bear something of the mantle of authority, Marguerite was a child with six parents instead of the usual two. Perhaps her portrayal of Benjamin West in his large family of sisters and brothers reflects her own childhood status as the youngest in a devoted but well-disciplined family.
>
> (*My Little Sister, Marguerite Henry,* [OP])

There were many influences which gave stability and impetus to the writing career of young Marguerite. There was Papa, who "could yodel, sing folk songs, or recite whole passages of Shakespeare. Papa was a printer and his shop was a wondrous place," wrote Marguerite. Papa's printing plant was visited on Saturdays. "Presses whirred. Long sheets of paper streamed out of them. They went in clean and came out covered with words. Papa's desk was more exciting than Pandora's box. It yielded big fat tablets in pink, green, yellow and blue, and bundles of pencils that write in a big black swathe. No thin, gray, inconspicuous lines came out of Papa's pencils. Everyone noticed when Papa wrote" or when he yodeled, or sang or recited.

Gertrude continues: "Papa never said, 'A penny for your thoughts.' Always it was, 'A tablet for your thoughts.' At home we filled the tablets with stories and verses, as highly colored as the paper on which they were written. When at the age of eleven Marguerite sold one of the stories to the old *Delineator Magazine,* the rejoicing in our family almost equaled our pride later over her first accepted book."

Marguerite writes about her mother: "We lived in a modest little house in Milwaukee and no youngster had a happier period of growing up.... Mama wore starched white shirtwaists and carried her head like a thoroughbred. When she went to a party, we all danced attendance. One found her hand-bag, another brought her hat, her coat. In snow-time we brought out her boots and put them on for her. We were proud of Mama."

Marguerite wrote her way through high school and two years of Milwaukee State Teachers College, but romance and marriage interrupted her formal education. Her sister Gertrude recalls that "as a bride, settled in a small apartment in Chicago, she helped her husband get out his sales bulletin, wrote technical articles for trade journals, visiting manufacturing plants and making minute observations of complicated processes. The more complicated her subject, the more she seemed to delight in boiling it down into simple, understandable English, and the more the demand there was for her work.... Eventually she found her way into the *Saturday Evening Post* with a series of 'Turning Points in the Lives of Famous Men'."

When the Henrys moved out of the city into a cozy cottage in the country, Marguerite discovered that "writing for children was the kind of writing she had always wanted to do." Of course animals, and especially her enthusiasm for horses, and the detail of their care, now that she had a place to keep them, prompted her first stories and her first research into some of the unique horses of America.

How does an author work when she is as careful a researcher as Mrs. Henry has become? Big Sister, Gertrude Jupp, describes the process:

> I think Marguerite has a unique way of working. Instead of making an outline for her stories she used a whole riffle of Manila folders, filling them with notes listing what people wore, what they ate, how they lived in the period of her story. The folders are boldly labeled in black crayon and are separated into two groups — those with the plot incidents in their natural progression and those containing background material. One glance at the big black labels gives her a quick visual outline.
>
> Besides taking detailed notes, she often has photostats made of scenes from source books. She surrounds herself with these and other pictures to put herself into the mood and setting of her story. Above her desk is a bulletin board covered with scenes of races, court ceremonies and children, dogs and horses.

Over the years in her writing career, Mrs. Henry has received many awards for her more than 20 children's books. But as her sister indicates, "just as highly treasured as these recognitions, however, are the letters which come to Marguerite Henry from boys and girls."

It is her success with young readers — and their response to her stories and her treatment of people and animals that have a real history which makes Mrs. Henry really unique as a writer today. What other modern writer receives so many thousands of letters from her readers that she has had to publish a book in order to try and answer the questions which come pouring into her mailbox? It is the way in which Mrs. Henry answers these questions which gives us one of our best studies of her own character and convictions.

First published in 1969 as *Dear Readers and Riders,* the book then appeared in a Rand McNally paperback as *Dear Marguerite Henry* by Marguerite Henry [OP]. It is a book of some 220 pages, complete with index. It includes, in addition to the reprinting of the letters and their authors, the answers and a generous selection of Mr. Wesley Dennis' illustrations — those illustrations which have made their collaboration such an excellent teamwork over the years. There are some actual photographs, too, and a few snapshots of the author. It is a book to delight and inform readers and riders — of all ages.

The questions range widely, from some individuals who desire to obtain, when they grow up, some of the fine types of horses about which Mrs. Henry has written, and from others asking about the writing and researching process. A few letters venture to question statements of fact about specific horse types. These she graciously corrects or she corroborates their statements. Helpfully, the book is divided into chapters pertaining to many of the books she has written and the questions directed to specific books and horse breeds are dealt with accordingly.

The personal questions about the author, her husband, her animals, her illustrator, Mr. Wesley Dennis, are handled with open tact and taste — so much appreciated in this age of crudity and indelicacy. It is a wholesome book by a whole-souled woman.

Three Marguerite Henry Books Recommended for You to Read

Here are three books which are especially interesting about historic personages and animals. They provide excellent teaching material and can be used as a book to read aloud to your family or class, to develop their listening-learning skills. They can be used by a class where each student has an individual copy of the book. The Benjamin West book has a teaching syllabus available from F.A.C.E. that has been developed for the Notebook Approach, an aspect of teaching by Principles (American Christian method).

Robert Fulton, Boy Craftsman by Marguerite Henry, Childhood of Famous Americans series, Bobbs-Merrill (1945), recently reprinted by Mile-Hi Publishers.

The political liberty of the American Colonies, gained as a result of their separation from England, and their willingness to pray their way through a seven-year war for independence, began a new era in the world. Now there was opportunity for the contribution of talent in the fields of science and invention so that the young American nation might become self-sufficient in trade and manufacturing.

THE CLERMONT

Robert Fulton was a young American who began to figure out how to do necessary jobs more efficiently. He invented a machine for spinning flax, and a machine for making rope, and a mill for sawing marble. He learned how to design guns while working for the local gunsmith who also served the community as a blacksmith. Later on, while studying art under Benjamin West in England, Robert Fulton turned to the work for which he had been preparing — the perfection of the steam engine. In 1807 he developed the first American steamboat named the "Clermont." Fulton's work enabled enterprising Americans to travel the rivers and the newly constructed canals which were binding the nation together. His work increased the trade and traffic around America.

From the *Journals of Washington Irving* we learn how much he appreciated the invention of the steamboat. After an absence from America for seventeen years, he returned in 1832 and traveled up the Hudson River to his beloved Catskill Mountains. He continued to the Niagara Falls, and then across Lake Erie to Detroit. Other trips were down the Ohio River to the Mississippi as he proceeded to Fort Gibson, and west. Thus the waterways and canals provided the steamboat travelways for Americans.

The *Robert Fulton* book is an excellent reader for schools that are endeavoring to return to a more wholistic approach of learning. It enables you to give your students an opportunity for learning in depth — rather than the smattering which is often the only source of study. Best of all it provides you with a mirror of early America.

It was while she was writing her book on Robert Fulton that Mrs. Henry discovered the Quaker Painter from Penn's Colony, Benjamin West, Father of American Painting. Her book **Benjamin West and His Cat Grimalkin,** Bobbs-Merrill (1947),** is a prize resource for teaching and learning. It is also one of the most charming books about our first internationally known American Artist. Self-taught, as were most of our early painters, Benjamin learned how to make his colors from his Indian friends. He obtained his first hair brush from the tail of his pet cat, Grimalkin.

by Wesley Dennis

In addition to a delightful story, well told, and well illustrated by Wesley Dennis, Mrs. Henry has given us a vivid picture of Quakers in the colony settled by William Penn. The Middle colony of our Parent Colonies, was a Proprietary grant given by the King to Penn. The Quaker character prevailed for some 100 years and it is this character which we see in Papa West and his family of five sons and five daughters and their Inn and farm in Pennsylvania of the seventeen hundreds. Mamma is the love and support for Benjamin.

This book is too rich to be wasted just as a reading book. It is much more rewarding if taught carefully so as to expand the knowledge and the enjoyment of teaching and learning our American History and character. Our suggestions for teaching it at home or to an entire class are developed in our teaching syllabus for the notebook approach.

A third book which we value for its identification of American character as a result of our American Christian Constitution is, ***Justin Morgan Had a Horse*** by Marguerite Henry

(1954), Macmillan.* Here again we see how even a horse can testify to the uniqueness of American liberty and opportunity during the pioneer days of our nation in Vermont. In her Foreword to the book Mrs. Henry has written:

> This is the story of a common, ordinary little work horse who turned out to be the father of a famous family of American horses. He lived in the Green Mountain country of Vermont in the days when America was growing up. In fact, he helped it grow up. He dragged logs and cleared land. He helped build the first log houses. He helped build bridges and cut roads through the wilderness.
>
>
> *by Wesley Dennis*
>
> Even in his own lifetime, the willingness of this little horse became an American legend. He labored hard all day, and then at sundown, when he should have been fed and bedded down for the night, he took part in races and pulling-bees. He could walk faster, trot faster, run faster, and pull heavier logs than any other horse in all Vermont.
>
> Today his descendants, known as Morgan horses, are renowned throughout the world. Yet nobody knows whether that first Morgan's parents were British or French or Dutch. And nobody really cares. As Joel Goss figured it out: "He's just like us. He's American. That's what he is! American!"

This book will help your students to appreciate what kind of effort and persistence it takes to develop and establish an idea. But the story of the school-teacher, Justin Morgan, and his dream and realization of an all-purpose horse for Americans to work with was finally realized in the Morgan horse who had both strength and heart and became a loved horse for his owner.

WESLEY DENNIS

THE ARTIST MOST OFTEN ASSOCIATED WITH MARGUERITE HENRY

"Wesley Dennis, who worked so successfully as a 'team' with Marguerite Henry, was a genuine down-Easterner — born in Massachusetts and brought up on Cape Cod. He studied art in both the United States and Paris, and after several years of free-lancing decided that his real interest lay in country life, especially horses. In 1942 he wrote and illustrated his first juvenile book: *Flip, the story of a flying horse*. About the same time he began to illustrate a series of articles for hunting periodicals. Later he won acclaim as a highly successful and popular illustrator of juvenile books — especially vigorous out-of-doors stories. He illustrated most of the Marguerite Henry books, in addition to many by other writers and several of his own. Until his death in 1966, he lived near Warrenton, Virginia, where he carried on his painting and illustrating in the kind of surroundings he found most stimulating."

(From "About the Author and Artist," *White Stallion of Lipizza,* Rand McNally/Macmillan edition.)

BOOKS AND AWARDS
MARGUERITE HENRY, AMERICAN AUTHOR

DATE	TITLE; PUBLISHER	SUBJECT; PERIOD	AWARDS
1945	*Robert, Fulton, Boy Craftsman* Bobbs-Merrill; reprint, Mile-Hi	Early American Inventor	
1947	*Benjamin West and His Cat Grimalkin*, F.A.C.E.*	Penn's Colony. First American Painter.	Listed by Lib. of Cong., juvenile best expressing the American spirit.
1948	*Misty, of Chincoteague* Macmillan; F.A.C.E.	First volume dealing with the wild ponies on Assateague Island off Virginia's shore.	Lewis Carroll Shelf Award. Boys' Clubs of America.
1948	*King of the Wind, the Story of the Godolphin Arabian*, Macmillan	Beginning of the thoroughbred influence of Arabian horses on American horses.	Newbery Award
1949	*Sea Star, Orphan of Chincoteague* Macmillan	Virginia and the island of the wild ponies.	Young Reader's Choice — Pacific Northwest Library Association
1950	*Born to Trot* Macmillan	The Grand Circuit of Trotting Races, Horses, Owners and Trainers.	
1953	*Brighty of the Grand Canyon* Macmillan	Grand Canyon National Park and the story of a lone burro who played a part in its development.	William Allen White Award
1954	*Justin Morgan Had a Horse* Macmillan; F.A.C.E.	Development of the Morgan strain in Vermont and its inventor.	A Junior Literary Guild Selection. Friends of Literature Award
1956	*Cinnabar, The One O'Clock Fox* Macmillan	A red fox who lived in the time of George Washington and, says legend, challenged the General to a chase.	
1957	*Black Gold* Macmillan	A courageous thoroughbred who wins his race on three legs and a heart at Fair Grounds Park, New Orleans.	Sequoyah Children's Book Award
1960	*The Wildest Horse Race in the World*, Macmillan	The Palio Race in Siena, Italy.	Clara Ingram Judson Award
1962	*Five O'Clock Charlie* Macmillan	A Clydesdale horse who lived in Shropshire, England and was never late for tea.	Weekly Reader Children's Book Club Selections
1962	*All About Horses* [OP]	The history of horses. An instructive manual with photographs.	
1963	*Stormy, Misty's Foal* Macmillan	Chincoteague and the story of the disaster and the results of the huge storm.	
1964	*White Stallion of Lipazza* Macmillan	The story of the Vienna Spanish Riding School and the training of the Lipizzaner horses.	
1966	*Mustang, Wild Spirit of the West* Macmillan; F.A.C.E.	The story of "Wild Horse Annie" and her efforts to win a Nevada wild horse refuge.	Western Heritage Award. Sequoyah Children's Book Award
1969	*Dear Marguerite Henry* [OP]	Letters to Mrs. Henry and her answers to her readers and riders.	
1971	*Peter Lundy and the Medicine Hat Stallion* [OP]	Nebraska Territory 1850; a boy with a horse and its sacred head-markings.	
1975	*The Little Fellow* [OP]	For younger children, a picture book of a foal in bluegrass country.	
1977	*One Man's Horse* [OP]	A postlude to *Born to Trot* about Dutchman Rysdyk and his trotting horse, Hambletonian, progenitor of all great trotters in the world.	

*A teaching syllabus by Rosalie J. Slater is available with *Benjamin West*.

LEARNING TO TEACH THE PRINCIPLE APPROACH WITH THE ILLUSTRATED BIOGRAPHIES BY INGRI AND EDGAR PARIN D'AULAIRE

AMERICAN AUTHORS
Ingri (1904–) and Edgar (1898–) Parin d'Aulaire

> ...America adopts the children of all lands only to return a manhood ennobled by a sense of its own dignity through the practice of a system of self-government which improves the condition and promotes the interest of each while it produces harm to none. (Hall, *Christian History,* VOL. I, p. 8)

America, made up of individuals from all nations and continents, and belonging to all races, does indeed adopt many children, who, in turn, enrich America by their contributions of character and talent.

The d'Aulaires, a talented husband-and-wife team, both write and illustrate books for younger children. Ingri was born and educated in Norway. Edgar came from Switzerland where his father was famous as a portrait painter. They met in Paris, both students of art, and eventually they came to America. They decided, like so many millions of other individuals, that America should become home for them. Anne Carroll Moore, a well-known Children's Librarian, suggested that they combine their talents and produce beautiful books for children — so they began.

At first Ingri and Edgar Parin d'Aulaire wrote books about other nations — but gradually they began to choose American individuals for their highly illustrated biographies. Among these are the following, listed in order of their historical chronology, not in the order of their production by the authors. The books are printed by Bantam Doubleday Dell.*

Columbus (1451–1506)
Pocahontas (1595?–1616)
George Washington (1732–1799)
Benjamin Franklin (1706–1790)
Abraham Lincoln (1809–1865)
1939 Caldecott Medal

At first glance, one might believe that the color, vitality, and joy, which is immediately evident in the d'Aulaire illustrations, is intended to portray historical figures without respect for character. A sense of comedy seems almost suggested by their stylistic figures. But this is not so. In actual fact, all of the biographies are carefully researched. The d'Aulaires do careful study and reading both on the historical period in which their subject lived and on the life and character they are representing in their illustrations and text. Then they actually travel to the locations of the historical events connected with each individual biography.

While working on their book *Columbus* the d'Aulaires spent two years collecting materials and visiting every spot which they describe and illustrate. This included trips to the Old World — to Italy and to Spain, gathering their historical and artistic data. They sketched, visited, and made notes on the spot. Then they traveled back to the New World locations in the Caribbean. Here they sailed to the actual islands discovered by Columbus and met some of the last descendants of those Carib Indians with whom Columbus had so many dealings.

Samuel Eliot Morison, maritime biographer of Christopher Columbus, wrote:

> Most biographies of the Admiral might well be entitled: *"Columbus to the Water's Edge."* The authors either care little about the Discoverer's career on his chosen element, or expended so much space on unprofitable speculation about his birth, character and early life that no room was left to tell where and how he sailed. (Preface, *Admiral of the Ocean Sea: A Life of Christopher Columbus*)

Morison, an admiral in his own right, organized the famous Harvard Columbus Expedition of 1939–40, and re-sailed all of Columbus' four voyages. He would have appreciated the efforts of the d'Aulaires to authenticate their work by physical as well as mental research. In fact, most of us would have liked to join with them on their interesting and colorful voyages of research and rediscovery.

THE ART OF THE D'AULAIRES

The rich and colorful individuality of Ingri and Edgar Parin d'Aulaire as artists is especially interesting. Many of the d'Aulaire fine illustrated volumes bear this inscription: "The drawings for this book were lithographed directly on stone by the artists and lithographed in four colors in the United States of America." Some volumes are lithographed on stone in five colors. Actually, the d'Aulaires were the first artists in this country who returned to their early method of painting and craftsmanship.

Noah Webster, in his 1828 *American Dictionary of the English Language,* defines *lithography* as follows:

> LITHOGRAPHY *n. (Greek origin combining stone and to engrave or write.)*
> The art of engraving, or of tracing letters, figures, or other designs on stone, and of transferring them to paper by impression; an art recently invented by Mr. Sennefelder of Munich, in Bavaria.

In *The Lincoln Library of Essential Information,* 33rd Edition, The Frontier Press, Columbus, Ohio (1970), there is the following:

> *Lithographic stone.* A smooth, porous, even grained and compact variety of limestone. When a flat surface of such a stone is marked with a design in soapy ink or crayon, moistened, and then passed under an inking roller, the ink from the roller is retained only by the material forming the design. The process of printing from a stone treated in this manner is known as *lithography....* Lithographic stones of the finest quality are obtained at Solnhofen, Bavaria. In limited quantities, lithographic stone occurs in France, England and America.

In the United States the most important deposit is at Brandenburg, Kentucky. See *Limestone*."

The d'Aulaires have stylized many elements of their illustrations. This means that, except for the main characters, the figures suggest but do not represent. For instance, in their *Columbus* volume, all the Indians and all the sailors look alike but conform in design. The main subjects of the biographies, however, are distinguishable and their individuality is consistent throughout.

The pages of the d'Aulaire volumes are filled with designs and figures suggesting the historical period of the main character and subject of the biography. Perhaps the most exact are those in the *Franklin* volume as they are from the Pennsylvania Dutch. Also included on each page is a wise saying from Franklin's *Poor Richard's Almanac*.

Despite stylization in the d'Aulaire illustrations there is great charm in their composition and drawing. We are always drawn to their subjects in warm appreciation. In *Columbus* we feel the drama of his discovery and of his trials and ordeals afterwards. In *Pocahontas* we perceive from the first her sympathy for the Jamestown settlers and her interest in them which explains her efforts to help them to survive. *George Washington* contains compositions of home and plantation settings which are harmonious and satisfying to study. *Franklin* is the most ingenious of the books — but so is the main character. And *Abraham Lincoln* contains the most exaggeration in drawings of the main character — perhaps to suggest his effect upon those who beheld him.

In the 1939 Caldecott Medal, awarded each year in the United States for the finest illustrated children's book, the d'Aulaires were finally recognized. The name of the medal is derived from Randolph J. Caldecott (1846–1886), an English illustrator of children's books. Today a number of Caldecott books have been reprinted for our enjoyment.

The selection of books for children to be incorporated into the program is based upon a basic philosophy of American Christian Education. We will discuss the application of The Principle Approach in the teaching of these books and indicate the references and the resources available for parents and teachers who are working at the unity of all subjects through the Christian History Program.

LEARNING TO TEACH CHRISTOPHER COLUMBUS
WITH THE PRINCIPLE APPROACH

Leading Idea:

Christopher Columbus is a Providential Link in the Westward Move of the Gospel and individual liberty under Constitutional Government.

Leading Questions:

What events take place in Europe to prepare the impetus towards America — one hundred years before Columbus? *Principle:* Which is causative, the *internal* or *external*? What will be the distinct contribution of Columbus under God's direction and Purpose? What will *not* be his role?

American Christian Philosophy of Education and Government

All teaching and learning begins with the following steps:

Biblical Research:

To understand the Providential History of any event, individual, or subject field, we need first to know Biblical History and God's stated purposes for men and nations. What preparation principles are at work? What is the relationship of the study of Christopher Columbus to Biblical History?

Historical Research:

Our Historical Setting is always the Chain of Christianity moving Westward to American with the liberty and responsibility of the individual. What Providential events in history do we see at the time of Columbus? What preparations are being made in a number of fields which will be helpful for this voyage?

- Religious Preparations
- Scientific Preparations
- Governmental Preparations

What prominent individuals are contributors to the greatest voyage in history — that of Columbus?

Geographical Research:

What is the geographical knowledge of the times? Do we see God's Hand at work in this field? What roles do *Portugal* and *Spain* play in exploration and geographical research? Who is *Prince Henry the Navigator*? What is the influence of Marco Polo's travels to China upon Columbus?

BANNER OF COLUMBUS' EXPEDITION

Christian History Principles:

Which principles of self- and civil government are seen in the life and character of Christopher Columbus? What principles of religion and government are reflected in the lives and character of Ferdinand and Isabella?

References and Resources

In order to prepare to teach *Christopher Columbus* at any level the parent or teacher needs to begin their own voyage of discovery and exploration in order to set forth the course which they will want to teach. But we have rich resources at our disposal so that our own curriculum will be Biblically, historically, educationally based. All subjects will be unified in the philosophy and should reflect the individuality and diversity of the teacher. A revitalized curriculum will flow from a *re*vitalized teacher — a teacher whose own character has grown and developed spiritually and academically. Students with such a teacher can also be directed and inspired to become productive learners — relating his or her academic education to the development of talents and testimony.

Teaching and Learning:

Teaching and Learning America's Christian History: The Principle Approach, by Rosalie J. Slater (1965), Foundation for American Christian Education.

See page 305 in *Teaching and Learning* for steps in teaching a course. See page 307 for the discussion of *Step Four: Questions for Invention,* and page 309 for *Step Six: Original Thought.* Those steps in teaching and learning indicate how teachers and students can make application to their own lives of every new aspect of Christian History they learn.

Books for Researching for Teachers and Students:

Christopher Columbus's Book of Prophecies and *Christopher Columbus, His Life and Discovery in the Light of His Prophecies* by Kay Brigham, Libros CLIE, Barcelona (1992).

The Travels of Marco Polo, Yule Edition, Airmont Classics (CL186).*

Marco Polo by Gian Paolo Ceserani (1977), The Putnam Publishing Group.

Prince Henry the Navigator and the Highways of the Sea by Thomas Caldecot Chub (1970), The Viking Press, New York [OP].

The European Discovery of America, Vol. 1, S.D. 500-1600; Vol. 2 1492–1616. (Vol. 1 includes the Northern Voyages, Vol. 2, Southern Voyages), by Samuel Eliot Morison, Oxford University Press.

Biographies:

Admiral of the Ocean Sea, A Life of Chistopher Columbus by Samuel Eliot Morison (1942), Little, Brown and Company, Boston.

History of the Reign of Ferdinand and Isabella the Catholic by William H. Prescott, 1890 edition, [OP].

Christopher Columbus and the Discovery of the New World by Josephine Pollard (in Words-of-One-Syllable, for elementary and high school); reprinted by The Pilgrim Institute, Granger, IN; [OP].

Maps:

George F. Cram, Inc., Indianapolis. Map No. 503 or 1023 (same map), *Voyages and Discoveries in 1610.*

LEARNING TO TEACH
CAPTAIN JOHN SMITH AND PRINCESS POCAHONTAS
WITH THE PRINCIPLE APPROACH

CAPTAIN JOHN SMITH

Leading Idea:

Without the work of Captain John Smith and the Princess Pocahontas in the preservation of the Colony of Jamestown "the present United States of America might never have come into existence."

Leading Questions:

In the Chain of Christianity, when did England become interested in the colonization of North America? What unique preparation did Captain John Smith consider was of the Hand of God for his work in America? Can you explain the dramatic change in the life of a Powhatan Indian which affected the life of a colony?

American Christian Philosophy of Education and Government

All teaching and learning begins with the following steps:

Biblical Research:

When does the Providential History of America begin? How is America's Christian History related to Biblical history and God's purpose for men and nations?

Historical Research:

When and by whom was England's first claim made to North America? What part does the Spanish Armada play in the settlement of Jamestown? What contribution do the following make to our parent colony?
– Queen Elizabeth
– Sir Walter Raleigh
– Richard Hakluyt
– Alexander Whitaker
– John Rolfe

FORM OF RALEIGH'S SHIPS

Christian History Principles:

Which of the Christian History principles are seen in the life of Captain John Smith? in Pocahontas? What principles of religion and government are visible in the Jamestown Colony? What is Captain Smith's remedy for the colony? What is his greatest contribution? What does the life of Pocahontas demonstrate?

References and Resources

The Christian History of the Constitution: Christian Self-Government by Verna M. Hall, "History of Virginia," pp. 150A–175

Teaching and Learning America's Christian History by Rosalie J. Slater. "Christian Self-Government in Virginia...," pp. 190–194; "Comparision of Self-Government in the Parent Colonies," pp. 197–200

Adult Books:

The Three Worlds of Captain John Smith by Philip L. Barbour, Houghton Mifflin (1964). A complete modern study of the fulness of Smith's background and life as it relates to our early colonization and his influence upon Pocahontas and the Jamestown colony, and upon the Pilgrims.

Captain John Smith's America edited by John Lankford (1967), A Harper Torchbook TB 3078, Harper Collins. Selections from the writings of Captain John Smith, the first writer of Virginia, including his description of New England.

Pocahontas by Grace Steele Woodward (1969), University of Oklahoma Press.* Written by an anthropologist, this book is a classic study of events which can only be explained by America's Christian History.

Children's Books:

John Smith, Man of Adventure by Miriam E. Mason (1958), A Piper Book, Houghton Mifflin Company, [OP]. This book provides excellent material for students and should be reprinted. Look for it in your library.

Pocahontas by Ingri & Edgar Parin d'Aulaire (1946), Bantam Dell Doubleday.* Illustrated biography, well researched and beautifully illustrated. You must provide the Christian base.

POCAHONTAS *by Ingri & Parin d'Aulaire*

Maps:

George F. Cram Company, Inc., Indianapolis. No. 503 or 1023 (same map), *Voyages & Discoveries to 1610.* No. 506, *Early Grants and Origin of the Thirteen Colonies.* Virginia and the Chesapeake Bay Region are important to study as this was the region of the Powhatan tribe of Pocahontas and was explored by Captain John Smith.

LEARNING TO TEACH GEORGE WASHINGTON WITH THE PRINCIPLE APPROACH

Leading Idea:

"Never before did such destinies hang on a single man, for it was not the fate of a continent which rested on the issue of the struggle, but of human liberty the world over." God's Providential preparation of men and nations for His Story.

Leading Questions:

In the education of George Washington what evidence do we see of God's Hand in particular fields of his preparation?

American Christian Philosophy of Education and Government

All teaching and learning begins with the following steps:

Biblical Research:

The study of Biblical History reveals God's purposes for men and nations. In the time of George Washington he was called the "Moses of America." Why did our American Christian colonists and historians refer to him in this way? What had they learned from their study of the Scriptures?

Historical Research:

In our historical setting of the Chain of Christianity moving westward to America we study the Discovery, Exploration, and Settlement of the Colonies. Then came some 150 years of practice in self-government as God prepared the colonies for nationhood. What are some of the particulars — men, events, writings, etc. — which were taking place during the youth and manhood of George Washington? Some things to consider:

- Life in Colonial Virginia and its government
- The French & War
- The Role of the Clergy
- Home life and education of George Washington
- Military and Governmental preparation
- Mount Vernon and George Washington

Christian History Principles:

Which of the Christian History Principles are instilled into George Washington's home life and education? What governmental principles are being practiced in Virginia? What was the relationship of church to state?

References and Resources

Children's Books:

The Life of George Washington in Words of One Syllable by Josephine Pollard. Reprinted by Mile-Hi Publishers, Denver, CO. This 1893 edition is an excellent history of the life of George Washington, covering the War for Independence and briefly his presidency. For good readers from Second Grade up.

Meet George Washington by Joan Heilbroner (1964), a Step-Up Book from Random House, Inc. A simply-told biography with well-researched illustrations.

George Washington by Ingri & Edgar Parin d'Aulaire (1987), Bantam Dell Doubleday. Illustrated biography.

Adult Books:

The Making of George Washington by General William H. Wilbur (1973), Patriotic Education, Inc., Alexandria, VA. This little book is a gem, for it is the only book available which describes the education of George Washington in detail and the influence of his father and brother Lawrence upon him. It can be used as a background study for teachers and for students beginning in the 4th grade. The Christian significance is dealt with but really must be provided by the teacher by his or her additional research in the Christian History volumes.

WASHINGTON *by Ingri & Parin d'Aulaire*

A Family Study on the Life of George Washington From America's Traditional Method of Biblical Reasoning, Home Study Guide for Parents by Belinda Beth Ballenger, Noah Webster Educational Foundation, Livermore, CA. This is an excellent 127-page guide to the study of General Wilbur's classic, *The Making of George Washington.*

The Christian History Books:

The Christian History of the Constitution of the United States of America: Christian Self-Government by Verna M. Hall, Foundation for American Christian Education, San Francisco, CA, "American Leadership," pp. 411–417.

The Christian History of the American Revolution: Consider and Ponder by Verna M. Hall, Foundation for American Christian Education; see "Index of Leading Ideas" for George Washington references.

"Washington and Lafayette: Two Men, Two Revolutions," by Rosalie J. Slater, *Journal of F.A.C.E.,* Vol. VI, pp. 103–153.

George Washington: A Collection, by E. B. Allen.

Maps:

George F. Cram Company, Inc., Indianapolis, IN. Maps Nos. 506, 507, 508, 509 deal with the early claims and grants and origins geographically of the 13 colonies. Give clear and graphic picture. Nos. 11 and 12 deal with the American Revolution in the Middle and Northern Colonies and in the South and West.

LEARNING TO TEACH BENJAMIN FRANKLIN WITH THE PRINCIPLE APPROACH

Leading Idea:

"He who makes the times go over us, has always the men ready to meet them...." Benjamin Franklin, 1706–1790. "American Statesman, scientist, philosopher, found by God for the new nation." (Hall, *Consider and Ponder,* pp. 52a; 648a)

Leading Questions:

Why was Benjamin Franklin the symbol of 18th century America to the rest of the world? What method of education — a method which became the American way of education — was the key to his success?

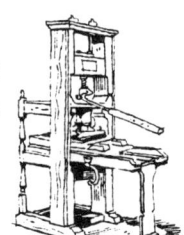

FRANKLIN'S PRESS

American Christian Philosophy of Education and Government

All teaching and learning begins with the following steps:

Biblical Research:

The Bible shows God's use of men of many talents and convictions for His purposes. The liberty in the American Colonies, even before Independence and because of its Christian base, enabled many men to serve their nation for the cause of civil and religious freedom. Franklin was just such a man.

Historical Research:

In the setting of the Chain of Christianity there was a time for America to come out as a separate nation under God. How did the Colony of Pennsylvania provide a unique setting for God's preparation of Benjamin Franklin to serve this nation at home and abroad?

Trace Franklin's early training and education. What one of his publications became a household item and made him famous throughout the world? What is read today of his works? What public benefits to Philadelphia did Franklin bring about? What example did he set for American communities? What was Franklin's most famous invention and how did it reflect the spirit and purpose of America? Why is Franklin called "the man who tamed lightning? What was its most immediate practical application in America? For many years Franklin served his nation away from home. What were his most important diplomatic contributions? What were his most important contributions governmentally?

Christian History Principles:

Which principles are best expressed in Franklin? What particular contributions did he make to our American Christian way of life?

References and Resources

The Autobiography of Benjamin Franklin, Houghton Mifflin Co. [OP]; Penguin USA; Random House; Macmillan. This is one of the most significant "self-lives" in our history, by a man whose contribution was highly visible on both sides of

the Atlantic. It should inspire all those who recognize that our American education has to be largely — self-education.

The Man Who Dared the Lightning by Thomas J. Fleming (1971), William Morrow and Company [OP]. A most complete and interesting biography of Franklin and a good description of his relations with the son who was a Royalist Governor of New Jersey. A positive biography of the Franklin character.

Juvenile Biographies:

Benjamin Franklin by Ingri & Edgar Parin d'Aulaire, The Putnam Publishing Group.

Meet Benjamin Franklin by Maggi Scarf (1868), a Step-Up Book from Random House, Inc. This is a well-told biography in 60 readable pages.

Maps:

The George F. Cram Company, Inc., Map No. 509, *The Thirteen Colonies 1760–1775,* an excellent map covering our pre-revolutionary era. Map No. 11, *The Revolution in the Middle and Northern Colonies,* shows battles in the early part of the war, chiefly along the Hudson and Delaware Rivers. Map No. 12, *The Revolution in the South and West,* shows such campaigns as George Roger's march and the retreat of Cornwallis to Yorktown.

LEARNING TO TEACH ABRAHAM LINCOLN WITH THE PRINCIPLE APPROACH

Leading Idea:

"With malice toward none; with charity for all; with firmness in the right, as God gives us to see the right, let us strive on to finish the work we are in; to bind up the nation's wounds; to care for him who shall have borne the battle, and for his widow, and his orphan — to do all which may achieve and cherish a just, and a lasting peace, among ourselves, and with all nations." (Lincoln's 2nd Inaugural Address, March 4, 1865)

Leading Questions:

What were the major purposes which God raised up Abraham Lincoln to fulfill in his Presidency? How can we evaluate the influence of his public service?

American Christian Philosophy of Education and Government

All teaching and learning begins with the following steps:

Biblical Research:

What might Abraham Lincoln have studied in the Bible of the qualities of character which men should express — especially those qualities required of men who hold public office? How is the principle of Property developed in the Bible and what are its distinctions from Old Testament time to the New Christian era?

Historical Research:

The period of Lincoln's public life and service falls in our decline from our early character and principles. Can you outline our Colonial and Constitutional periods and indicate when this period begins? What were the leading causes of our falling away from our Christian and Biblical foundations? What were the causes of the Civil War? Were they external or internal?

Christian History Principles:

Which of the Christian History principles do you see in the life and character of Lincoln? What principles are especially tested by the Civil War? What aspects of Lincoln's life and presidency were Christian? What does the Lincoln Memorial celebrate of his character and contribution to the nation?

References and Resources

Adult Books:

Writings and Speeches by Abraham Lincoln.

There are many biographies and studies of Abraham Lincoln.

Abraham Lincoln: The Man and His Faith by G. Frederick Owen, Tyndale House; an available Christian biography of Abraham Lincoln.

The Glory and the Dream, Abraham Lincoln, before and after Gettysburg by Michael A. Musmanno, The Long House.

Children's Books:

Abraham Lincoln by Ingri and Edgar Parin d'Aulaire, The Putnam Publishing Group.*

ABRAHAM LINCOLN

Abe Lincoln Grows Up by Carl Sandburg (1926), Illustrated by James Daugherty, A Voyager Book, 1975 edition published by Harcourt Brace Jovanovich;* taken from the massive two-volume study of Lincoln by Sandburg, *Abraham Lincoln, the Prairie Years.*

Abraham Lincoln: God's Leader by David R. Collins, Mott Media. A Christian biography of Lincoln.*

Meet Abraham Lincoln by Barbara Cary, a Random House Step-Up Book. Covers the life and service of Lincoln in 86 pages for young readers.

Maps:

George F. Cram Company, Inc. Map No. 518, *The United States in 1861* on the eve of the Civil War, free and slave states that seceded. Map No. 519, *The Civil War 1861–1865*, area where war was fought and campaigns.

THE AMERICAN INDIAN IN OUR LITERATURE

And God blessed them, and God said unto them, Be fruitful, and multiply, and replenish the earth, and subdue it: and have dominion over the fish of the sea, and over the fowl of the air, and every living thing that moveth upon the earth. And God said, Behold, I have given you every herb bearing seed, which is upon the face of all the earth, and every tree, in the which is the fruit of a tree yielding seed; to you it shall be for meat. And to every beast of the earth, and to every fowl of the air, and to every thing that creepeth upon the earth, wherein there is life, I have given every green herb for meat: and it was so." (Genesis 1:28,29)

Stewardship of the earth and the mandate to be productive and bring forth fruits were the responsibility of man. But without the Bible primitive man could not know of his individual responsibility.

When the Jamestown settlers were in want because of their unwillingness to plant corn, determined rather to search for gold, the Indians through trade supplied them. The Princess Pocahontas, impelled by God to sustain them, often brought supplies to Jamestown and later, after her conversion to Christianity, instructed her husband John Rolfe in principles of tobacco planting.

But for the most part the Indians of the Eastern Coast were not farmers. The men did not believe in working in the fields and turned over this responsibility to the women. Only after the missionary work of John Eliot and Daniel Gookin did newborn Indian men begin to accept work as a natural and scriptural responsibility.

The Indians of the Southwest, especially those denoted Pueblo Indians, were among the few Indian tribes who worked at farming in a sustained fashion. But these Indians were not known to Americans for many years after the forming of the nation.

So it is not surprising that our French visitor, Alexis de Tocqueville in his study of *American Institutions and Their Influence,* wrote that at the time of the European discovery of America, "the Indians occupied, without possessing it."

Richard Frothingham in *The Rise of the Republic of the United States* (1890), Little, Brown, and Company, (p. 5) [OP], observed that "neither the exuberance of the soil, nor the magnificence of the rivers, nor the influence of the climate, nor the geographical conditions that stimulate commerce, rouse in them the capacity to develop the resources of this splendid country." The Indians did not know of, nor could they pay "heed to any divine command to subdue and replenish the earth."

Missionary Work Among the Indians

Yet from the first the goal of English colonization was the evangelization of the Indians on the American continent. The Princess Pocahontas was the first fruit of Jamestown, largely through the friendship of Captain John Smith and the spiritual direction of Virginia's great apostle, Alexander Whitaker. But Pocahontas, or Rebecca Rolfe, was an exception, and the work of evangelization lagged for so long, that in 1622, the Powhatan Indians massacred many colonists at Jamestown.

In Massachusetts Bay Colony for almost sixty years Pastor John Eliot ministered to the Indians. Traveling through the forest paths on foot or horseback, teaching the Indians in their own language, he produced the first American Bible — in Algonquin. There were many critics of the work of evangelization of the Indians — both white and red. But John Eliot and Daniel Gookin helped set up fourteen Praying Towns in Massachusetts which the Indians governed and supported. In 1675 King Philip's War threatened to end the missionary work. Yet when the Christian Indians joined forces with the white men the tide was turned and the devastating war ended. Once again the work of evangelization went on and a second edition of the Bible was published.

The most difficult challenge which has faced America with her Indians has been their own desire to remain outside the American nation. While many Indians have made the transition into American life the majority have wished to keep their original lands and maintain a primitive existence. Christianity alone has the answer as to how these problems can be solved and the principle of unity with diversity maintained. It will take a true understanding of the American Christian Philosophy of Government and the Biblical principles underlying them to reconcile the differences. America should always be "one nation under God" — with that unity with diversity which has made her so unique under our Constitution.

American Indians in Our Literature

The Christian influence upon the Indians as seen in our literature begins with the conversion of the Princess Pocahontas. John Smith's writings on the General History of Virginia reflect his many experiences with the Powhatan Tribe in Virginia and his friendship with Pocahontas. And Alexander Whitaker's Christianization and civilization of Pocahontas are also a testimony to God's Work. Many books and plays and poems have been written about Pocahontas whose baptism picture graces our Capitol building in Washington, D.C. among other historic paintings.

The Pilgrims in Plymouth enjoyed almost fifty years of peace with the Patuxet Indians and through their great friendship for Chief Massasoit. Samoset, Squanto, Hobomok and others were fine friends of the Pilgrims who endeavored to bring the Indians under the protection of the Plymouth laws. Beginning with William Bradford's great classic, *History 'Of Plimoth Plantation,'* and with Edward Winslow's *Good News From Virginia,* there is heartening documentation about the Pilgrims and the Indians. There are still some books available about the Pilgrims.

John Eliot and Daniel Gookin and other Puritans in Massachusetts Bay recorded their Christian work with the Indians. But there is little to read to our children today for the records are in the historical societies and in limited editions.

Jonathan Edward's biography of *David Brainard, Missionary to the Indians,* is also a source for the courage and character of a man whose heart longed to bring Indians' souls to the Lord. However, there are no editions readily available to read to the next generation.

The Individuality of the Red Man

There are some books which identify those terrifying periods in American History when white settlers were faced with Indian raids and attacks. These attacks occurred during the seventeenth century and during the eighteenth, when the European powers were making a last attempt to hold American ground. Particularly in that period of the 1750s of the French and Indian War when the French used certain tribes in their warfare against the English, do we have some frightening records.

The character of the American Indian, until touched by Christ, remained uncivilized. Our first American novelist, James Fenimore Cooper, in his Leatherstocking Saga of five novels dealing with the American wilderness, identified the individuality of the white and red races. Each race was true to its "gifts." The barbarian Indian might scalp — for that was his custom. But the white man might not carry out the same barbaric custom — for it was not according to his "gifts." Cooper's remarkable classics *The Deerslayer* and *The Last of the Mohicans* became our finest tribute to the understanding of this diversity. His main character in the Leatherstocking tales is an American Christian woodsman whose fair dealings with the Indians teach us much about our opportunities to maintain our own Biblical character and conscience.

There is much literature in which the American Indian plays a role. It is important to choose wisely with a background of America's Christian History and Government. The principle of unity with diversity must be maintained. America must remain "one nation under God" in order to fulfill her purpose to propogate the Gospel principles of internal and external liberty to all men and women.

THE CAPTIVITY AND RESTORATION OF MRS. MARY ROWLANDSON

On the tenth of February, 1675, came the Indians in great numbers upon Lancaster. Their first coming was about sun-rising. Hearing the noise of some guns, we looked out: several houses were burning, and the smoke ascending to heaven. There were five persons taken in one house; the father, the mother, and a suckling child they knocked on the head; and the other two they took and carried away alive....

Thus begins the account told by Mary Rowlandson, "the devout helpmate" of Lancaster's first ordained minister. "Her simply told tale was the earliest literary composition by a citizen of the town... it is also an invaluable contribution to early New England history."

This unique "pathetic record of grave perils bravely encountered, and terrible sufferings patiently borne with an unswerving faith in the wisdom and mercy of an overruling Providence was first issued from the press in 1682." We quote briefly from the 1930 reprint of this early edition, by Houghton Mifflin Company, entitled *The Narrative of the Captivity and Restoration of Mrs. Mary Rowlandson.... Who was taken Prisoner by the Indians...written by her own hand....*

Mrs. Rowlandson, after recording some of the terrible sights of the attack stated:

I had often before this said, that if the Indians should come, I should choose rather to be killed by them, than taken alive; but when it came to the trial, my mind changed; their glittering weapons so daunted my spirit, that I chose rather to go along with those (as I may say) ravenous bears, than that moment to end my days. And that I may better declare what happened to me during that grievous captivity, I shall particularly speak of the several Removes we had up and down the wilderness.

The First Remove

Now away we must go with those barbarous creatures, with our bodies wounded and bleeding, and our hearts no less than our bodies. About a mile we went that night, up upon a hill within sight of their town, where they intended to lodge.... This was the dolefulest night that ever my eyes saw. Oh the roaring and singing and dancing and yelling of those black creatures in the night, which made the place a lively resemblance of hell.... To add to the dolefulness of the former day, and the dismalness of the present night, my thoughts ran upon my losses and sad bereaved condition. All was gone, my husband gone (at least separated from me...), my children gone, my relations and friends gone, our house and home and all our comforts within door and without, all was gone, except my life, and I knew not but the next moment that might go too. There remained nothing to me but one poor wounded babe, and it seemed at present worse than death, that it was in such a pitiful condition, bespeaking compassion, and I had no refreshing for it, not suitable things to revive it...."

The Second Remove

But now, the next morning, I must turn my back upon the town, and travel with them into the vast and desolate wilderness, I knew not whither... but God was with me in a wonderful manner, carrying me along, and bearing up my spirit, that it did not quite fail.... Then they set me upon a horse with my wounded child in my lap, and there being no furniture upon the horse's back, as we went down the steep hill, we both fell over the horse's head at which they like inhuman creatures laughed, and rejoiced to see it, though I thought we should there have ended our days, overcome with so many difficulties. But the Lord renewed my strength still, and carried me along that I might see more of his power; yea, so much that I could never have thought of, had I not experienced it.

After this it quickly began to snow and when night came on they stopped. And now I must sit down in the snow before a little fire, and a few boughs behind me, with my sick child in my lap, and calling much for water, being now (through the wound) fallen into a violent fever. My own wound also growing so stiff that I could scarce sit down or rise up; yet so it must be that I must sit all this cold winter night upon the cold snowy ground, with my sick child in my arms, looking that every hour would be the last of its life, and having no Christian friend near me, either to comfort or help me. Oh, I may see the wonderful power of God, that my spirit did not utterly sink under my afflictions; still the Lord upheld me with his gracious and merciful spirit, and we were both alive to see the light of the next morning...."

The Third Remove

> ...Thus nine days I sat upon my knees with my babe upon my lap.... My child being even ready to depart this sorrowful world, they bade me carry it to another wigwam, (I suppose because they would not be troubled with such spectacles), whither I went with a very heavy heart, and down I sat with the picture of death in my lap. About two hours in the night my sweet babe, like a lamb, departed this life, on February 18, 1675, it being about six years and five months old. It was about nine days from the first wounding in this miserable condition, without any refreshing of one nature or another, except a little cold water.... In the morning when they understood that my child was dead, they sent for me home to my master's wigwam.... I went to take up my dead child in my arms to carry it with me, but they bid me let it alone: there was no resisting, but go I must and leave it. When I had been (awhile) at my master's wigwam, I took the first opportunity I could get to go look after my dead child. When I came I asked them what they had done with it. Then they told me it was upon the hill, then they went and showed me where it was, where I saw the ground was newly digged, and there they told me they had buried it. There I left that child in the wilderness, and must commit it, and myself also, in this wilderness condition to him who is above all...."

Later Mrs. Rowlandson received a Bible to help her through this terrible experience.

> I cannot but take notice of the wonderful mercy of God to me in those afflictions, in sending me a Bible. One of the Indians that came from the Medfield fight had brought some plunder, came to me, and asked me if I would have a Bible. He had got one in his basket. I was glad of it and asked him whether he thought the Indians would let me read [it]. He answered, yes. So I took the Bible and in that melancholy time it came into my mind to read first the 28th chapter of Deuteronomy, which I did. And when I had read it my dark heart wrought on this manner: That there was no mercy for me, that the blessings were gone and the curses came in their room and that I had lost my opportunity. But the Lord helped me still to go on reading, till I came to chapter 30, the seven first verses, where I found there was mercy promised again if we would return to him by repentence; and though we were scattered from one end of the earth to the other, yet the Lord would gather us together, and turn all those curses upon our enemies. I do not desire to live to forget this scripture, and what comfort it was to me....

Mercifully Mrs. Rowlandson was able to talk with her ten-year-old daughter and later found her son.

> Hearing that my son was come to this place, I went to see him and found him lying flat upon the ground. I asked him how he could sleep so. He answered me that he was not asleep but at prayer, and lay so that they might not observe what he was doing. I pray God he may remember these things now he is returned in safety.

Another blessing during the horrible weeks of travel and suffering was that Mrs. Rowlandson was not physically assaulted.

> I have been in the midst of those roaring lions and savage bears that feared neither God nor man nor the devil, by night and day, alone and in company, sleeping all sorts together, and yet not one of them ever offered the least abuse of unchastity to me in word or action. Though some are ready to say, I speak it for my own credit; but I speak it in the presence of God, and to his glory. God's power is as great now, and as sufficient to save, as when he preserved Daniel in the lion's den, or the three children in the fiery furnace. I may well say as his Psalm cvii. 1,2 *Oh give thanks unto the Lord for he is good: for his mercy endureth for ever. Let the redeemed of the Lord say so, whom he hath redeemed from the hand of the enemy,* especially that I should have come away in the midst of so many hundreds of enemies, quietly and peacefully, and not a dog moving his tongue....

Redemption Rock, after twenty removes and months of direful captivity, was the place, upon which was engraved these memorable words:

REDEMPTION ROCK, PRINCETON

UPON THIS ROCK MAY 2nd 1676

WAS MADE THE AGREEMENT FOR THE RANSOM

OF MRS. MARY ROWLANDSON OF LANCASTER

BETWEEN THE INDIANS AND JOHN HOAR OF CONCORD

KING PHILIP WAS WITH THE INDIANS BUT

REFUSED HIS CONSENT

Having lost her home, but returned to her husband and with her remaining children, the Rowlandsons were provided for until they finally settled in Connecticut. She concluded:

> Thus hath the Lord brought me and mine out of that horrible pit and hath set us in the midst of tender-hearted and compassionate Christians. It is the desire of my soul that we may walk worthy of the mercies received, and which we are receiving.... The Lord hath been exceeding good to us in our low estate, in that when we had neither house nor home nor other necessities, the Lord so moved the hearts of those towards us that we wanted neither food nor raiment for ourselves and ours; Proverbs xviii 24, *There is a friend that sticketh closer than a brother.* And how many such friends have we found, and now living amongst! ...
>
> I can remember the time when I used to sleep quietly without working in my thoughts, whole nights together, but now it is otherwise with me. When all are fast about me and no eye open but his who ever waketh, my thoughts are upon things past, upon the awful dispensation of the Lord towards us, upon his wonderful power and might in carrying us through so many difficulties, in returning us to safety and suffering none to hurt us.... And I hope I can say in some measure, as David did, *It is good for me that I have been afflicted....*

BOOKS TO READ TO YOUR FAMILY ABOUT THE INDIANS

The Matchlock Gun by Walter D. Edmonds, Illustrated by Paul Lanz (1941), Dodd, Mead & Company [OP].

This is the true story of the Van Alstynes, Dutch settlers in the Hudson Valley in 1756 when the French and Indians were endeavoring to dislodge the English settlements. In the history of liberty God had enabled the Dutch to overcome the Spanish invaders in their land so when Edward's great-grandfather came to America he brought with him a matchlock or Spanish gun.

> See, Edward, it's a matchlock. It doesn't fire itself like the musket, with a flint. You have got to touch the priming with fire, like a cannon.

Called away from home to watch for marauding Indians who were burning the upper New York State settlements, Edward's father, Teunis Van Alstyne, rode away leaving his little family to wait and watch. After a few days, Edward's mother, Gertrude, felt the Indians were near them and they got down the big Matchlock gun, loaded and primed it — "and with all her flatirons propped the gun so that it pointed to the missing corner of the blind straight out onto the steps of the stoop." Surprised by the Indians in her garden patch, Gertrude was forced to run for her life shouting to her son *"Ateoord!"*

What happened next is history. When Captain Teunis Van Alstyne returned he found his little family in the yard beside the burned down home. His wife, Gertrude, was still unconscious from her tomahawk wound, Trudy was asleep, and "Edward sitting up with the gun across his knees, the bell mouth pointing at the three dead Indian bodies."

The Courage of Sarah Noble by Alice Dalgliesh, Illustrated by Leonard Weisgard (1954), Macmillan.

This is the true story of Sarah Noble and her family. It happened early in the eighteenth century when Sarah's father traveled by horseback from Westfield, Massachusetts to New Milford, Connecticut. John Noble had bought land and he wished to build a house before he moved his family. Sarah came with him to cook for him. She was only eight years old but she wanted to help her father.

It is evident from the first chapter that the Nobles do not fear the Indians. There is a basis for this which is perceived as you read the story. Nevertheless Sarah does have temptations to be afraid. A basic theme of the book is, *Keep up your Courage, Sarah Noble.*

This charming account of one family's dealings with the Indians should be read aloud before children read it for themselves. Since the purpose of literature is to read ideas, ideals, and character, it is important to provide a background for discussion. Parent and teacher preparation in this regard are most important, for in discussing the characters in a book it is possible to relate emotions and feelings to our own lives. Literature is a most excellent resource which God has provided to "soften the soil" and to "plant good seed" in hearts and minds.

Leonard Weisgard, artist-illustrator, provides excellent detail in his careful brushstrokes and washes. We can clearly determine the individuality of both nature and man. Writers and illustrators can help us become more observant so that *having eyes we can see*. Mr. Weisgard has a fine feeling of harmony in his work which provides support to the author's themes and style.

Only thirty years separate the experiences of Mrs. Rowlandson and the Nobles and only fifty years later the Van Alstynes have their experience with the Indians in the Hudson River Valley.

America's Christian History of the Indians has many fine chapters. The Pocahontas story is memorable. And the Pilgrims' treaty with the Indians lasted almost fifty years while the Indians enjoyed the equality of the law in Plymouth. Pilgrims, Puritans, Quakers and many others made it a practice to purchase land from the Indians and not take it from them. On page 270 of *Christian History* is a black and white rendition of the famous painting by Benjamin West, *Penn's Treaty with the Indians*.

Note: A workbook on reading comprehension entitled *The Courage of Sarah Noble, Teacher* can be obtained from Mile-Hi Publishers.

The Deerslayer or The First War-Path by James Fenimore Cooper (1841), Penguin. Of all the authors who dealt with the American Indian in our literature, James Fenimore Cooper (1789–1851) has left us with a literary legacy which we can share with our children and students. Living for some years in Cooperstown, New York, he came to know well the region which later characterized his novels of the white man and the red man. In his main character of five novels entitled *The Leatherstocking Tales,* he contributed to American Literature a unique American Christian hero. Natty Bumpo became by virtue of his Christian character and prowess in forest ways, *Deerslayer, Hawkeye* or simply *Leather-Stocking*.

> The author has often been asked if he had any original in his mind for the character of Leather-Stocking. In a physical sense, different individuals known to the writer in early life certainly presented themselves as models, through his recollections; but in a moral sense this man of the forest is purely a creation.

by Frank T. Merrill

Could a man placed in the savage wilderness still conduct his life along Christian principles? While removed from temptations of civilization would he succumb to the lure of Indian ways and wisdom? Cooper is a fine exponent of God's Principle of Individuality for he, through Deerslayer, is true to what he identifies as "white gifts" and the "gifts" of the "red man." Respecting the best in the Delaware tribe that he has lived with, Deerslayer refuses to change his own identity and mix it with that of the red man. By being true to himself, as Shakespeare admonished, he remains true to the individuality of both races.

Leatherstocking, though illiterate, has been taught Biblical principles by the Moravians. His senses drink in the spiritual and he is aware of God's presence, power and beauty in Creation — especially in the unspoiled wilderness as yet untouched by man. While the Indians associated with Leatherstocking or Deerslayer are not Christian many of the tribes were evangelized. James Fenimore Cooper in his Preface to *The Leatherstocking Tales* states:

> The Delawares only attracted the attention of the missionaries, and were a tribe unusually influenced by their precepts and example. In many instances they became Christians, and cases occurred in which their subsequent lives gave proof of the efficacy of the great moral changes that had taken place within them.

Cooper's efforts to "picture red men both as heroes and villains" naturally met with criticism in his day and ours. But he respected the work of the Moravian Missionary, John Heckewelder (1743–1823). Born in England, he became a preacher, came to America in 1754, and began his benevolent labors with the Indians of Pennsylvania, a task of some forty years. "He studied carefully their language, manners, and customs,...established himself at Bethlehem, one of the principle Moravian establishments in North America. His knowledge of the Delaware tongue caused his frequent employment to accompany pacific missions among the Indians.... Becoming members of the Philosophical Society of Pennsylvania they published their 'Transactions, a History of the Manners and Customs of the Indian Nations'... and a year later in 1820, 'A Narrative of the Mission of the United Brethren Among the Delaware and Mohegan Indians.'" (*Dictionary of American Biography Including Men of the Time*, 1872)

Cooper commented on the criticism of his treatment of the red man:

> It has been objected to these books that they give a more favorable picture of the redman than he deserves.... One of his critics, on the appearance of the first work in which Indian character was portrayed, objected that "its characters were Indians of the school of Heckewelder, rather than of the school of nature." These words quite probably contain the substance of the true answer to the objection. Heckewelder was an ardent, benevolent missionary, bent on the good of the redman, and seeing in him one who had the soul, reason, and characteristics of a fellow-being.

A special edition of *Deerslayer* and *The Last of the Mohicans*

In 1911 one of the great publishing houses, Charles Scribner's Sons in New York, began publishing a series known as "Scribner Illustrated Classics." Their first book was *Treasure Island* by Robert Louis Stevenson. What distinguished this series were the unique illustrations by Newell Convers Wyeth, who signed his paintings "N.C. Wyeth." Wyeth was the product of an unusual school in Wilmington, Delaware, the Howard Pyle School of Art. A leading American illustrator and author, Pyle, by his character and teaching, restored the interest and accuracy in painting which made our history and literature come alive through the illustrations of his students.

For over thirty years N.C. Wyeth was commissioned to illustrate many of these Scribner Illustrated Classics. Two of them were by James Fenimore Cooper and these editions are worthy of reading — and possibly owning, if you can find them in old bookstores at a price you can afford.

Indians of the Southwest

Among the most interesting Indians in America are the desert Indians or Indians of the great Southwest of Utah, Arizona, Colorado, and New Mexico. There have been many sympathetic studies and stories about the Pueblo and Navajo Indians. Today the Navajo Tribes maintain the individuality of their nation and it is possible to visit their celebrations and dances and purchase some of their beautiful rugs and pottery. The Pueblo Indians, too, still maintain some of their ancient crafts and make exciting excursions to the ancient dwellings of these cliff and desert people.

Maria: The Potter of San Idlefonso by Alice Marriott, a trained ethnologist and author, University of Oklahoma Press. This is a beautiful study, written for adults, and is the actual account of Maria Martinez and her husband Julian who revived the ancient Pueblo craft of pottery-making and the development of the unique black-on-black ware. The literary style of the author permits us to become part of Maria's world — so that we feel a kinship to these Indians and anticipate knowing more about them.

In My Mother's House by Ann Nolan Clark, illustrated by Velino Herrera [OP]. Ann Nolan Clark has written a number of books about our desert Indians. She was at one time a teacher of Southwestern Indian children and one who caught the spirit and beauty of their lives. Perhaps her most delightful book entitled *In My Mother's House* best introduces us to this land of little rain, much sand, and a people sensitive to maintaining their own identity. The book is written in rhythmic prose which sets it apart as unique. Its illustrations are simply line drawings, some in color, which are direct, accurate, and pleasing. The last page summarizes the content of the book:

The pueblo,
The people,
And fire,
And fields,
And water,
And land,
And animals —
I string them together
Like beads.
They make a chain,
A strong chain,
To hold me close
To home,
Where I live
In my Mother's house.

Mrs. Clark has also written about the Navajo Indians in *Little Navajo Bluebird* [OP].

Dancing Cloud and *Hah-Nee,* by Mary and Conrad Buff [OP]. Mary and Conrad Buff lived among the Indians and have several beautifully-illustrated and beautifully-written books on the desert Indians, especially *Dancing Cloud* and *Hah-Nee* (both out-of-print). Because they are illustrators first they convey much by their desert paintings and endeavor in their texts to interpret the spirit of the Indian mind and heart.

Waterless Mountain by Laura Adams Armer (1931), David McKay, Co., Random House.

Laura Adams Armer, a Californian, spent time as a painter studying the Navajo Indians in Northern Arizona. Her interest in their folklore produced a prize-winning book for young people, *Waterless Mountain*. This book requires more preparation on the part of the reader to understand the legends, traditions, and mysticism of the Navajo, but it is faithfully written in order to represent these unique Indians.

NAVAJO FAMILY
The American Indian by Sydney E. Fletcher

A California Indian Story

Island of the Blue Dolphins by Scott O'Dell (1960), Newbery Winner, Houghton Mifflin Company.

In the 1800s a twelve-year-old California Indian girl was marooned on one of the farthest Channel Islands off the Coast of Santa Barbara. This true story of her eighteen-year survival on the island, and her return to the Santa Barbara Mission, is both a realistic and resourceful tale of courage and serenity.

Scott O'Dell, distantly related to Sir Walter Scott, is a native Californian and well qualified by his study of California history to write this story. He writes:

> In that year the Spanish explorer Sebastian Vizcaino set out from Mexico in search of a port where treasure galleons from the Philippines could find shelter in case of distress. Sailing north along the California coast, he sighted the island, sent a small boat ashore and named it La Isla de San Nicolas, in honor of the patron saint of sailors, travelers, and merchants....
>
> The girl Robinson Crusoe whose story I have attempted to recreate actually lived alone upon this island from 1835–1853, and is known to history as The Lost Woman of San Nicolas....
>
> The Lost Woman of San Nicolas is buried on a hill near the Santa Barbara Mission. Her skirt of green cormorant feathers was sent to Rome.

The Island of the Blue Dolphins is one of the eight Channel Islands, some of which are seen from Santa Barbara. One of the outermost islands, San Nicolas may one day be swept back into the sea for it is in the path of pounding waves and furious winds.

LITERATURE OF THE BIBLE LANDS

Across the Valley of Kidron spread the massive walls and huddled houses, the towers and domes of Jerusalem. As I stood on the Mount of Olives, gazing upon this Holy City of three great faiths, I thought of its momentous past. Here, tradition says, Abraham prepared to sacrifice his son Isaac. Here rose the City of David, and here Solomon built his temple in the days of Israel's glory. I could almost hear the tinkling of the Queen of Sheba's caravan — camels bearing "spices, and very much gold, and precious stones" — shuffling soft-footed into Solomon's resplendent capital.

Here Jesus walked during His last days. I saw the gleaming Dome of the Rock, site of Herod's Temple where Jesus scourged the money changers. Below me, gnarled olive trees in the Garden of Gethsemane reflected Jesus' agony. On Mount Zion, far to my left, stood the traditional Room of the Last Supper. In the distance ahead, I picked out the Church of the Holy Sepulcher, enshrining the place where He fulfilled His promise to "give his life as a ransom for many." I thought:

If only there were a book that could capture the power of this scene, that could bring Bible times to life as did my own journey to Bible lands.

(*Everyday Life in Bible Times,* Foreword by Melville
Bell Grosvenor, National Geographic Society, 1967)

One hundred years ago few Americans could expect to visit the Holy Land. The voyage by ship was lengthy and expensive and accommodations in the Middle East were primitive. Yet many Americans became *armchair travelers* to Bible lands through books. Also, Bible Study of the nineteenth century included a study of the geography and history of the area and archeology made its contribution as the century closed.

Between the years 1868 and 1886 the field of archeology came dramatically alive through the efforts of one man with a dream. Heinrich Schliemann, a German merchant and self-taught archeologist, began a series of excavations on classical sites in Greece and Asia Minor. Schliemann was a Homer enthusiast. He had practically memorized Homer's *Illiad* and *Odyssey,* and he dreamed of finding the fabled city of Troy. His well-publicized discoveries, his colorful and forceful personality, and his unorthodox adventures into the field roused the attention, if the not the wrath, of scholars who scorned his methods. Schliemann's adventures are excellent reading for young people as well as adults and fortunately there are two biographies available:

The Walls of Windy Troy, A Biography of Heinrich Schliemann by Marjorie Braymer (1960), Harcourt, Brace & World, A Voyager Book, 176-page juvenile, [OP].

The Greek Treasure, A Biographical Novel of Henry and Sophia Schliemann by Irving Stone (1975), Bantam Doubleday Dell.

Biblical archeology had long been exploring the sites of the Old and New Testaments, but it was officially launched in 1890. At the same period a new field was launched in literature which made it possible for readers to travel with the mind's eye and imagination to the Bible Lands.

Up to 1880 no novel had been written with Jesus Christ as a central figure. But in 1880 an American author published what was to be the greatest Christian novel of all times — one which would faithfully portray the sights and scenes of the Middle East.

Lew Wallace was born in Indiana in 1827 when John Quincy Adams was President of the United States. The Erie Canal had just been completed and nine years later American settlers reached Oregon. America was still expanding from "sea to shining sea." David Wallace, Lew's father, became Governor of Indiana when Lew was fourteen and served also in the House of Representatives. Mr. Wallace's interest in his children's home education included Reading Aloud to them from history and literature. This was to have a memorable influence upon his son Lewis.

Lew Wallace became a lawyer, and the youngest Major General in the Union Army during the Civil War. He was present during many critical events of these years and distinguished himself. But it was while serving as Governor of the New Mexico Territory, dealing with Apache Wars and the capture of the outlaw, Billy the Kid, that he began work on the major novel of his life. Published in 1880, *Ben Hur, A Tale of the Christ,* was the first literary work to make Jesus Christ a central figure. Up to that time the American public would have considered it blasphemy. But *Ben Hur* became a powerful testimony of Jesus Christ. Lew Wallace himself, through the writing of the novel, came to accept Him as his Saviour and Lord.

An outstanding feature of *Ben Hur* was its careful research and description of the geography and settings of the novel. Lew Wallace did not visit the Middle East until after the publication of the book. In 1881 he was appointed Minister to Turkey and it was at this time that he visited for the first time the lands which formed the background of *Ben Hur.* Wallace was surprised to see how remarkably accurate he had been and found no need to rework any part of the novel. It is this reality and authenticity which had made *Ben Hur* so satisfying to its readers and which has proved a challenge to the many stage and screen versions of the novel.

Ben Hur became a standard for all future writers of adult and children's novels of Biblical setting at the time of Christ. In 1895, Mrs. Annie Fellows Johnston, famous for her delightful stories of a Kentucky girl called *The Little Colonel,* wrote her own children's Christian classic, entitled *Joel: A Boy of Galilee,* with Jesus Christ as a central figure. In her preface, Mrs. Johnston acknowledges the influence of *Ben Hur* on her writing:

> In this volume, it has been the purpose of the author to present to children, through "Joel," as accurate a picture of the times of the Christ as has been given to older readers through *Ben Hur.* With this in view, the customs of the private and public life of the Jews, the temple service with its sacerdotal rites, and the minute observances of the numerous holidays have been studied so carefully that the descriptions have passed the test of the most critical inspection. An eminent rabbi pronounces them correct in every detail.
>
> While the story is that of an ordinary boy, living among shepherds and fishermen, it touches at every point the gospel narrative, making Joel, in a

natural and interesting way, a witness to the miracles, the death, and the resurrection of the Nazarene.

It was with the deepest reverence that the task was undertaken, and the fact that the little book is accomplishing its mission is evinced not only by the approval accorded its first editions by so many, from Bible students to bishops, but by the boys and girls here and in distant lands.

Joel: A Boy of Galilee by Annie Fellows Johnston, published in 1895 by L. C. Page & Company, Boston, was out-of-print for many decades. Now *Joel* has been republished by the Foundation for American Christian Education, in paperback with new illustrations, so that we can restore to American Christians the reading of this quality book aloud in their homes and schools.

To give present-day American Christians some of the flavor of the quality of children's books in the Bible Lands setting, here is a short episode from *Joel: A Boy of Galilee:*

> Over on the horns of Mount Hattin, the spring morning began to shine. The light crept slowly down the side of the old mountain, till it fell on a little group of men talking earnestly together. It was the Preacher of Galilee, who had just chosen twelve men from among those who followed Him to help Him in His ministry.
>
> They gathered around Him in the fresh mountain dawn, as He pictured the life in store for them. Strange they did not quail before it, and turn back disheartened. Nay, not strange! For in the weeks they had been with Him, they had learned to love Him so, that His "follow me," that drew them from the toll-gate and fishing-boat, was stronger than ties of home and kindred.
>
> Just about this time, Phineas and Joel were starting out from Capernaum to the mountain. Hundreds of people were already on the way; people who had come from all parts of Judea, and beyond Jordan. Clouds of dust rose above the highway as the travelers trudged along.
>
> Joel was obliged to walk slowly, so that by the time they reached the plain below, a great multitude had gathered.
>
> "Let's get close," he whispered. He had heard that those who barely touched the garments of the strange Rabbi were made whole, and it was with the hope that he might steal up and touch Him unobserved that he had begged Phineas to take him on such a long, painful walk.
>
> "There is too great a crowd, now" answered Phineas. "Let us rest here awhile, and listen. Let me lift you upon on this big rock, so that you can see. 'Sh! He is speaking!"
>
> Joel looked up, and, for the second time in his life, listened to words that thrilled him like a trumpet call.... Joel forgot the press of people about him, forgot even where he was, as sentence after sentence seemed to lift him out of himself, till he could catch glimpses of lofty living such as he had never even dreamed of before....
>
> "Ye have heard that it hath been said, 'An eye for an eye and a tooth for a tooth.'"
>
> Joel started so violently at hearing his own familiar motto, that he nearly lost his balance on the rock.
>
> "But I say unto you that you resist not evil; but whosoever shall smite thee

on thy right cheek, turn to him the other also.... Ye have heard that it hath been said, Thou shalt love thy neighbor, and hate thine enemy. But I say unto you, Love your enemies, bless them that curse you, do good to them that hate you, and pray for them which despitefully use you, and persecute you."

Poor little Joel, it was a hard doctrine for him to accept! How could he give up his hope of revenge, when it had grown with his growth till it had come to be as dear as life itself?

He heard little of the rest of the sermon, for through it all the words kept echoing, "Bless them that curse you! Do good to them that hate you! Pray for them which despitefully use you!"

"Oh, I can't! I can't!" he groaned inwardly.

"I have found a chance for you to ride home," said Phineas, when the sermon was over, and the people began to file down the narrow mountain paths. "But there will be time for you to go to Him first, for healing. You have only to ask, you know."

Joel took an eager step forward, and then shrank back guiltily. "Not now," he murmured, "some other time." He could not look into those clear eyes and ask a blessing, when he knew his heart was black with hate.

After all his weeks of waiting the opportunity had come; but he dared not let the Sinless One look into his soul.

Phineas began an exclamation of surprise, but was interrupted by someone asking him a question. Joel took advantage of this to climb up behind the man who had offered him a ride. All the way home he weighed the two desires in his mind, — the hope of healing, and the hope of revenge.

By the time the two guardian fig-trees were in sight, he had decided. He would rather go helpless and halting through life than give up his cherished purpose.

But there was no sleep for him that night.... He thought of Jacob wrestling with the angel till day-break, and knew in his heart that the sweet spirit of forgiveness striving with his selfish nature was some heavenly impulse from another world.

At last when the cock-crowing commenced at dawn, and the stars were beginning to fade, he drew up his crooked little body, and knelt with his face to the kindling east.

"Father in heaven," he prayed softly, "bless mine enemy Rehum, and forgive all my sins, — fully and freely as I now forgive the wrong he had done to me."

A feeling of light-heartedness and peace, such as he had never known before, stole over him. He could not settle himself to sleep, though worn out with his night's long vigil.

Hastily slipping on his clothes, he tiptoed down the stairs, and limped bareheaded down to the beach. The lake shimmered and glowed under the faint rose and gray of the sky like a deep opal. The early breeze blew the hair back from his pale face with a refreshing coolness....

A firm tread on the gravel made him turn partly around. A man was coming up the beach; it was the friend of Phineas. As if drawn by some uncontrollable impulse, Joel started to meet Him, an unspoken prayer in his pleading little face.

Not a word was said. For one little instant Joel stood there by the shining sea, his hand held close in the hand of the world's Redeemer. For one little instant he looked up into His face; then the man passed on.

Joel covered his face with his hands, seeming to hear the still small voice that spoke to the prophet out of the whirlwind.

"He is the Christ!" he whispered reverently, — "He is the Christ!"

In his exulted feeling all thought of a cure had left him; but as he walked on down the beach, he noticed that he no longer limped. He was moving along with strong, quick strides. He shook himself and threw back his shoulders; there was no pain in the movement. He passed his hands over his back and down his limbs.

Oh, he was straight and strong and sinewy! He seemed a stranger to himself, as running and leaping, then stopping to look down and feel his limbs again, he ran madly on.

"NOT A WORD WAS SAID"

Suddenly he cast his garments aside and dived into the lake. Before his injury, he had been able to swim like a fish, now he reached with long powerful strokes that sent him darting through the cold water with a wonderful sense of exhilaration.

Then he dressed again, and went on running and leaping and climbing till he was exhausted, and his first wild delirious joy began to subside into a deep quiet thankfulness. Then he went home, radiant in the happiness of his new-found cure.

But more than the mystery of the miracle, more than the joy of the healing, was the remembrance of that moment, that one little moment, when he felt the clasp of the Master's hand, and seemed wrapped about with the boundless love of God.

From that moment, he lived but to serve and to follow Him.

(*Joel: A Boy of Galilee* by Annie Fellows Johnston, pp. 99–105)

For the Study of *Ben Hur*

Ben Hur: A Tale of The Christ — is currently out-of-print; find it in a library, find a used copy, or look for a new *unabridged* edition.

Teacher Guide for *Ben Hur: A Tale of The Christ,* Mott Media Publishing Co., [OP]. This 16-page guide has a number of helps to get you started in your study of the book including questions, discussion points, and test ideas. (See also The Noah Plan Literature Curriculum Guide from F.A.C.E.)

Lew Wallace, Boy Writer by Martha E. Schaaf, Bobbs Merrill [OP].

Everyday Life in Bible Times, National Geographic Society, [OP], provides an excellent background on the history and archeology of the Bible Lands with maps and illustrations. The chapter titles include "The World of Abraham, The World of Moses, The World of David and Solomon, The March of Empires, The World of Jesus, The World of Paul."

EVALUATING YOUR FAMILY READING ALOUD

RESTORING HOME AS THE EDUCATIONAL CENTER

As we stated in our section on the "American Christian Home" on page 3 of *Teaching and Learning America's Christian History: The Principle Approach,* the educational goal of home in our republic is to build the foundation of America's Christian character.

We know that in the home the foundations of Christian self-government are first learned and practiced.

And in the home, education begins the attitudes toward learning, toward study, toward the importance of "considering" and "pondering" — emphasis upon "reflective" living.

The Christian Home — A Teaching Ministry

Reverend S. Phillips, whom we quote at length on "The Christian Home" in *Teaching and Learning America's Christian History,* devotes much effort as a pastor to encourage his congregation to make home a teaching ministry. He says on page 20 of *Teaching and Learning,* "Many parents think that the office of teacher is not included in the parental character and mission. The neglect of home-training seems to arise out of an existing prejudice against it...."

Pastor Phillips deals with education in the home in all its critical functions which affect the community and the nation. He deals with Family Religion on page 8 of *Teaching and Learning:*

> Family religion includes parental Bible instruction, family prayer, and religious education, government, discipline and example.

Pastor Phillips deals with Home-Government on pages 23–26:

> The principle of home government is love — love ruling and obeying according to law.... This government implies reciprocity of right — the right of the parent to govern and the right of the child to be governed. It is similar in its fundamentals to the government of the state and church. It involves the legislative, judicial and executive functions; its elements are law, authority, obedience, and penalties. The basis of its laws is the Word of God.

Pastor Phillips deals with home education and he describes the function of books on pages 20–21:

> Give them proper books.... Bring them up to the habit of properly reading and studying those books. "A reading people will soon become a thinking people, and a thinking people must soon become a great people." Every book you furnish your child, and which it reads with reflection is "like a cast of the weaver's shuttle, adding another thread to the indestructible web of existence."
> ...Christian parents be faithful to this duty! Magnify your office as a teacher; be faithful to your household as a school. Diligently serve your children as the pupils that God has put under your care. Educate them for Him...."

We know that children *do not* learn how to "properly" read and study a book until they have watched and worked with their parents or teachers. Today our children *consume* many, many books. Yet they have not become "thinking" children. They have not been taught how to reason, how to relate, how to record. This is the challenge of the Family Program for Reading Aloud.

Parents — you do not realize how important you are to the education of your children. And, dear parents, you have such a wonderful educational treasure in reading, reasoning, and relating from books which you share with your children. Live with your children in the mental and emotional realm of books as well as you live with them in the physical realm of the homes, cars, and external advantages which you seek to provide for them. Children today are *deserted* by their parents in the areas where parents are most needed as teachers. Parents are *neglecting* their children — partly because they feel *inadequate* — because they have been poorly educated in history, in literature, in the arts and in science. But God has been merciful. He has provided you with four walls — a house, a home, an apartment, a cabin — where you can be alone with your family. Here no one will see you. No one can trespass upon your privacy. Here you can live and learn with your children as together you travel into the realms of mind, heart, imagination, and emotion — the internal, which is your primary area of responsibility and teaching.

Reflective and Non-Reflective Learning

American Christians have allowed our technological age to trespass upon the development of the American mind and character. We have allowed television to become the most intrusive technological influence of our times and it has affected the teaching and learning of our children.

Television is built upon Pavlovian Stimulus-Response of the consumer-watcher. (See *Teaching and Learning,* page 92 for Pavlov and the Non-Reflective Response.) As Jim Trelease writes in *The Read-Aloud Handbook* (revised 1985), Penguin USA: "Television is the direct opposite of reading. It requires and fosters a short attention span. Reading, on the other hand, requires and encourages longer attention spans in children." (p. 93)

We all know the frustration of the quick-fix plots and character development of television. There is no time to reflect on what is going to be the solution. There is not time to anticipate how an individual might respond, might challenge the events. Actually, the impersonality of television is its cruelest feature. It doesn't matter if we are watching. The individual is not needed. In Reading Aloud, on the other hand, the listener is most important, or should become most important to the Reader. Whether you are reading to one or to many, you should care as a Reader Aloud how the story is affecting the minds, the hearts, the imaginations of your listeners. And you should encourage discussion and anticipation. Let us *savor* our Reading Aloud — in our mind's eye. The Bible admonishes us: *Oh taste and see that the Lord is good.* (Psalm 34:8) This is not a physical tasting — but a spiritual — a mental tasting.

Mr. Trelease reminds us that *"Television deprives the child of his most important learning tool: his questions."* (p. 94) Many teachers teach without encouraging children to reason and to ask questions in discussion — before they record or write. As parents you can have some of your most enlightening times together with your children if you lead them down the paths of reason as a result of questions which your Reading Aloud should provoke.

"Television interrupts the most important language lesson in a child's life: family conversation," writes Mr. Trelease (p. 94). We know that today the art of conversation has all but disappeared around the family table, or in the living room with our guests. What can you do to restore this most important activity for the development of the reasoning and relating of ideas?

One thing which will help conversation is the family reading of books together which *inspire* conversation. Our Forefathers and Mothers read and discussed books which dealt with ideas and ideals, principles, in accord with God's Word. If we restore the level of our reading to books which will give us more substance, more character, and which relate to our importance in the perpetuation of American liberty — then our conversation level will rise.

Abigail Adams, Mercy Warren, and other wives and mothers of the American Revolutionary period, grew up in homes where conversation was an important avenue of learning. The women joined in and contributed to the conversation for they were, as John Adams defined them, "thinking" women, "reading" women.

In *The Women of the American Revolution* by Elizabeth Ellet, we learn how women educated their sons and daughters.

> The talk of matrons, in American homes, was of the people's wrongs, and the tyranny that oppressed them, till the sons who had grown to manhood, with strengthened aspirations towards a better state of things, and views enlarged to comprehend their invaded rights, stood up prepared to defend them to the utmost. Patriotic mothers nursed the infancy of freedom. Their counsels and their prayers mingled with the deliberations that resulted in a nation's assertion of its independence.... It is almost impossible now to appreciate the vast influence of women's patriotism upon the destinies of the infant republic." (Hall, *Consider and Ponder,* p. 73)

Establish Home Habits of Bible Study and Reading Together

It is startling to learn that we are not as well educated Biblically as were Americans of some one hundred years ago. In spite of the fact that there are larger churches and Sunday Schools, and despite the rapid growth of the Christian school movement, the Bible has not been extended to all of its spheres of influence. The simple fact is that, while we read and memorize Scripture faithfully, we are no longer, as a nation, individual students of the

Bible. Nor has our Christian education taught us how to research, reason, and relate Biblical principles into all fields of human life.

In our earlier *Family Program for Reading Aloud,* we included reference to a set of books which we had found helpful for Bible study. *The Book of Life,* arranged and edited by Newton M. Hall, A.M., D.D. and Irving F. Wood, Ph.D., D.D. and published from 1923 by John Rudin & Company, Inc., Chicago [OP], went through more than thirty editions. It was produced in the King James version, which was the highest level of the English language and was of the quality of language and expression of our English and American Literature. This was also the version which our Founding Fathers studied and no doubt was responsible for the high level of national literacy which preceded our Revolutionary and Constitutional periods.

The value of *The Book of Life* is that it encourages serious study of each section of the Bible which it reproduces with commentary. It also includes many of the masterpieces of the world's greatest art which portrayed Biblical scenes and characters. Our great hymns and the relationship of the Bible to literature is also identified. And, above all, the recognition of the Bible's relationship to government is clearly set forth, especially in the work of the Prophets, Bible Captains, Kings, and Statesmen.

Recently *The Book of Life* was purchased by a Christian publisher. Many of the original features of the set which were so rewarding to work with have disappeared. The format has been changed and expanded from eight or nine volumes to twenty. However, we believe that some of the original sets can be found — if you are willing to search patiently in the old bookstores. Perhaps you will be rewarded by finding a set which your family can still enjoy in your family Bible Study.

The Book of Life, arranged and edited by Newton M. Hall and Irving Francis Wood, published by John Rudin & Company, Inc., first printing 1923; this edition, 33rd (1972).

Book One: Doorway to the Bible
- My Bible Primer
- My Bible Reader

Book Two: Bible Treasures

Part One:
- In the Land of the Bible
- Little Journey in the Land of the Bible
- Stories of Old Testament Days

Part Two:
- A Child's Life of Jesus
- The Followers of Jesus
- The Story of the Hebrew People
- Persons of the Ancient Stories of the Hebrews
- Memory Verses for the Weeks of the Year
- Bible Dramas and Pageants
- Hymns and Poems

Book Three: Bible Heroes, Pioneers
- Stories of Ancient Days
- Stories of the Patriarchs
- A Nation in Bondage
- In the Wilderness
- The Book of the Law
- The Conquest of Canaan
- The Days of the Judges
- Ruth
- Hymns and Poems

Book Four: Bible Kings, Captains
- The United Kingdom
- The Divided Kingdom
- The Later History of Israel
- The Maccabees
- Esther
- Chronological Tables
- Hymns and Poems

Book Five: Bible Prophets, Statesmen
- The Prophets and the Exile

Book Six: Bible Poetry
- The Psalms
- The Book of Job
- Selections from the Book of Proverbs
- Selections from the Book of Ecclesiastes
- The Book of Lamentations
- Selections from the Song of Solomon

Book Seven: Life of the Master
    From the Gospels of Matthew, Mark & Luke
    From the Gospel of John
    Notes on the Gospels
    Sayings Ascribed to Jesus Outside the Gospels
    Beginnings of the New Faith
    Hymns and Poems

Book Eight: Paul, Life and Letters
    Paul the Great Captain of the New Faith
    The Letters of Paul, the Great Captain
    Letters of Leaders of the Early Church
    The Revelation of St. John the Divine

Book Nine: Bible Educator, Index
    The Bible in the Home and the School
    The Bible in English and American Literature
    Stories of the Hymns We Love
    The Apocrypha
    Indexes

FINDING TIME FOR GOD'S WORD

Ye do err, not knowing the Scriptures, nor the power of God.
[MATTHEW 22:29]

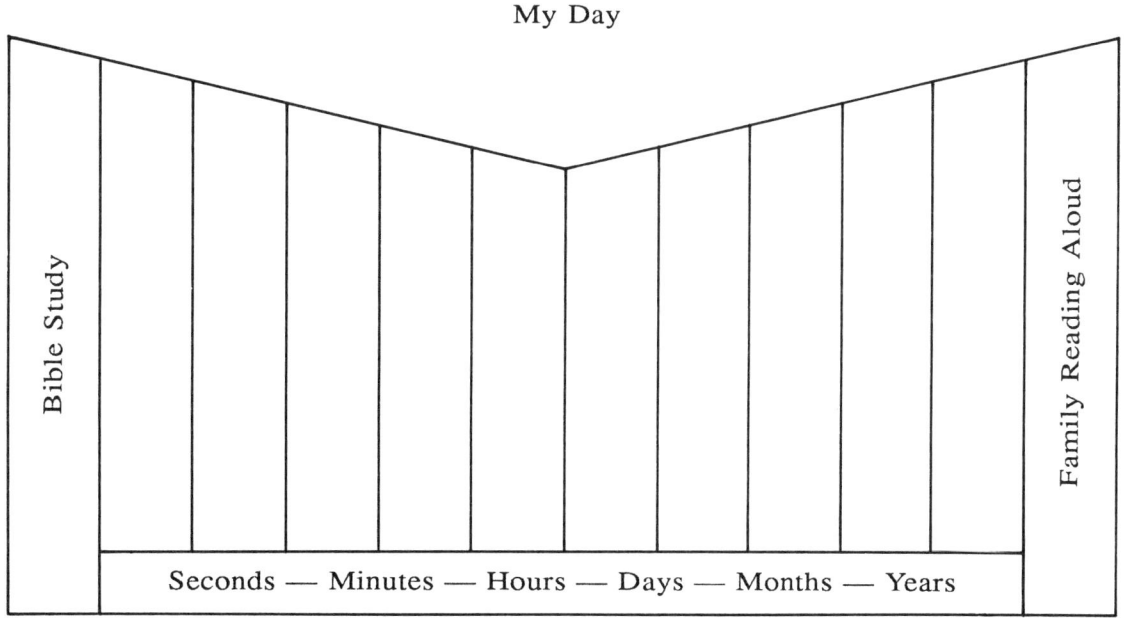

How My Day is Spent

Sleeping _____

Working/School _____

Church/Sunday School _____

T.V. Watching _____

Family Devotions _____

Family Bible Study _____

Family Reading Aloud _____

Other _____

A LESSON FROM THE WASHINGTON NATIONAL MONUMENT

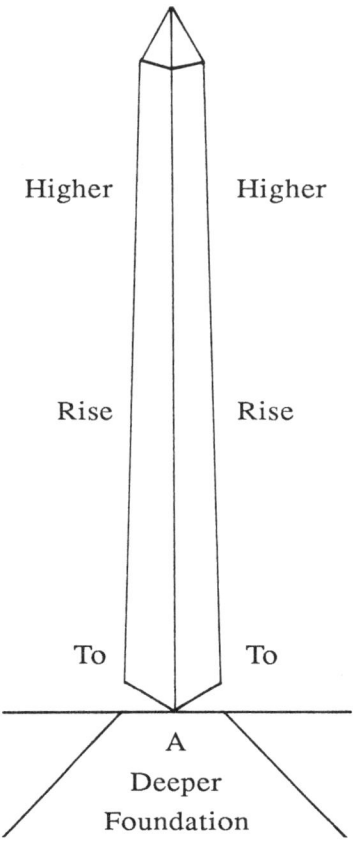

The most striking edifice to the eye in our nation's capital is the slim marble obelisk which rises some 555 feet high. Its story is one which should be studied for it took some 85 years to complete. Action to begin this memorial was started the day after the death of George Washington in 1799. But the cornerstone was not laid until July 4, 1848, and it was not dedicated until February 21, 1885. What caused the delay? One reason was disinterest and another, our *falling away*. But there was a structural reason, too. In 1873, after a lapse of 20 years when no building had occurred, it was found that the foundation was not sufficient to sustain the desired height. So began the work of strengthening and enlarging the foundation to carry the shaft to the desired height. The new foundation covers two and one-half times as much area and it extends 13½ feet deeper. The height is ten times the breadth. The lesson for us as individuals and as a nation is: if you wish to build higher you must deepen the foundations!

If the foundations be destroyed, what can the righteous do? [Psalms 11:3]

The "righteous" can rebuild the foundations.

LEARNING THE ART OF SELF-GOVERNMENT

Noah Webster speaks of *Habit* as "that which is the effect of custom or frequent repetition." Pastor Phillips indicates that habit is being established every day in the home — either good habits or bad habits. "Thus our habits become our masters, and are the irrevocable rulers of our life. This is true of good as well as of bad habits." (*Teaching and Learning*, p. 22)

If we are teaching our children *"the art of self-government"* we must be examples ourselves of consistent planning to include those "basics" — spiritual and intellectual — which we know to be as essential to our children as the meals which have become "the effect of frequent repetition" or habit in our homes.

In his chapter on *Family Habits*, Pastor Phillips gives direction to families on the importance of method and order in their daily lives (*Teaching and Learning*, p. 23):

> See, then, ye members of the Christian home, to the habits you are forming. Form the habit of *"doing all things decently and in order."* Let the work and duties of each day be done according to method. This is essential to success in your pursuits and aims.... You may have family prayer and instruction today, but something will prevent it tomorrow. Establish the habit of Christian industry. Be diligent; not slothful in business.... Establish the habit also of perseverance in well-doing. *"Be steadfast, immovable, always abounding in the work of the Lord."*

If you can order your home and habits to include daily Bible Study — you can order your home and habits to include daily Family Reading Aloud. This will take character — perhaps more character than any other aspect of home life. But if you begin to see results, if you can evaluate changes in attitudes, in the willingness to consider one's own character and disposition in the light of God's Word, this will be worth your efforts and determination. Above all, success with the "basics" in your children's lives will mean more to you than many of the activities which you have to give up in order to have time to read together, time to discuss, time to grow in grace.

May the Lord bless your efforts this year as you begin to take back the government and education of your own family.

If the foundations be destroyed, what can the righteous do? [Psalms 11:3]

The "righteous" can restore the foundations!

A FAMILY ACCOUNTING OF READING ALOUD

Who reads aloud to the family?
Father_____ Mother_____
Relatives_____ Others_____

Who listens to reading aloud?

Name	Age

How much time is spent in reading aloud?
Hours a Day_____ Hours a Week_____

How much preparation is made by the reader?
☐ Reading the book before you read it aloud   ☐ Researching some aspect of the book
☐ Travel in relation to the subject, either with the family or alone
_____
_____

What books have been read aloud to the family this year?

Author	Title

What have you learned about America through your family reading aloud?
_____
_____
_____
_____

What books have contributed to the development of Christian self-government in your family?
_____
_____
_____
_____

What new attitudes about the family have resulted from family reading aloud?
_____
_____

PART II

EXPANDING YOUR INTERESTS THROUGH READING IN DEPTH

INTRODUCTION

In *The Christian History Literature Program* many books are taught so that students may *unify* their learning and see the relationship of God and man and the unfolding of the events of the *history and character of liberty.*

But there are other purposes in the teaching and learning of literature. One of these purposes is to minister to the individual student. Through skillful teachers who are able to inspire and delight the mind and heart, new horizons are opened up, and new fields envisioned which provide challenge. The wider the range of reading, and the more focused, the greater are the opportunities for self-discovery.

But even if one does not discover a particular field of interest, wider reading allows for breadth and depth of vision and understanding. It can be a wonderful means of preparation for advanced learning and leadership. It builds bridges to other individuals than our own particular circle of friends.

Part II of our **Reading Aloud** is especially addressed to the High School years. Yet it is not exclusively designed for students. Many adults will want to begin to catch up with reading they never were interested in before. One might wonder why we classify these books under the term "Reading Aloud." While the bulk of reading at this level may be done individually, sharing one's reading interests with others often promotes the enjoyment of the book for oneself. It is a satisfaction to present something which inspires us and enables someone else to share in our enjoyment and insight. It is also true that when we read aloud we have to read more slowly than we read to ourselves. This often results in our paying more attention to aspects of the book which in our individual fast reading we might not have noticed. And of course a good book is like a piece of music. It has a tempo and a rhythm which becomes especially apparent when read aloud.

As you begin to look at the subjects we have chosen to present to you, we have started by sharing books which we enjoy in a certain field. All the books presented here are books which have inspired us for they deal with many *ideas and ideals,* and with *qualities of character* which we believe in. We mention a few books or *lead-ins,* and endeavor to present different *facets* of the same subject. In this way we hope to intrigue your own interests. You may want to read for an entirely different aspect than that which introduced us to the field. Our subjects may lead you to other related fields suggested by what we have outlined.

Look over our first five READING IN DEPTH areas. Select one subject area. Choose a book to read. As you discover the most *intriguing* aspect of the subject, present that aspect to someone else and learn their response. The purpose of reading in a specific field is to extend the horizons of our mind to contemplate the implications of a particular subject.

You may ask yourself — to what degree has my life been affected by this field? To what degree can I see the Hand of God here? Is there anything in this field to which I might make a contribution? What else might interest me in this area of life? Or, what ideas that lead into other subjects have been inspired by what I have read here?

If you keep a diagram, or *profile* of your wide reading, you may wish to add some of your reading discoveries to your record of exploration, or your ideas of what you would like to see happen in a particular field.

If any of the books mentioned below are not in your library, look up exact titles in *Books in Print,* then ask your library to obtain these books through inter-library loan. It can be done if you persist.

READING IN DEPTH

Choose an area of study and read *in depth* on this subject.

Choose an *author* who inspires or interests you and read *in depth* on that author. Read a number of writings by the author you choose.

Choose a *particular period of history* and read *in depth.*

The following are some examples of how you might conduct your *in-depth reading* and begin to build an individual *reading design* around some particular purpose for reading.

READING ON THE SUBJECT OF THE OCEAN

Matthew Fontaine Maury (1806–1873) was the Christian Founder of Oceanography. He was inspired by Scripture which refers to the sea: *"Whatsoever passeth through the paths of the seas."* (Psalm 8:8) Maury discovered the "paths of the seas" and in 1855 his charts and studies launched the field of Oceanography. Here are some references to his life and work both for adults and young readers.

ADULT REFERENCES:

Matthew Fontaine Maury: Scientist of the Sea, by Frances Leigh Williams, Rutgers University Press, 1963, (the definitive biography, fully documented with a bibliography of the many published works of Maury).

The Physical Geography of the Sea and Its Meteorology, by Matthew Fontaine Maury, John Leighly, Ed., republished by Belknap Press of Harvard University Press, 1963.

FOR YOUNGER READERS:

Ocean Pathfinder: A Biography of Matthew Fontaine Maury, by Frances Leigh Williams, Harcourt Brace and World, 1966.

The Pathfinder of the Seas: The Life of Matthew Fontaine Maury, by John W. Wayland, Garrett & Massie, Inc., Richmond, 1930.

OTHER ASPECTS OF THE OCEAN

The laying of the *Atlantic Cable,* which was helped by the work of Maury, can be found in two books by *Jean Lee Latham*: one, the biography of Cyrus Field, a major influence in the work of laying the cable; and two, Samuel F. B. Morse, also known for his work in telegraphy, sending the first message over the telegraph line in 1844 ("What hath God wrought?"), and American artist of note.

DIVING INTO THE OCEAN:

Commander Ellsberg has written three fascinating books on the work of recovery of treasure in his *Men Under the Sea, Thirty Fathoms Deep, Ocean Gold,* and others.

WHALING:

In our times every effort is being made to preserve these giant mammals of the sea — the whale. In order to appreciate how great the whaling industry was and how it provided New England men with a lifetime profession, read *Moby Dick* by Herman Melville. This is one of our great American classics. It is long, but it is a tremendous book about the contest between Captain Ahab, who has been wounded by the white whale, Moby Dick, and the whale itself. After reading this book you can expand your knowledge by finding some books about the efforts to protect and befriend the whale.

AMERICAN NAVY IN THE EARLY DAYS:

America's first naval heroes were men of courage and little experience. There are several books by William Bell Clark for young people as well as the series of volumes being published by our government edited and inspired by Mr. Clark's private collection of books and documents on our early navy. There are several adult and children's biographies available about John Paul Jones, our own pioneer in American Naval operations. Samuel Eliot Morison wrote an exceptional biography, *John Paul Jones: A Sailor's Biography,* 1959, Little, Brown, & Co.; republished in 1984 by Nebraska University Press.

Pictured here in battle is John Paul Jones' ship, the *Bonhomme Richard.*

Illustrated by Tom Dunnington
The Story of the Bonhomme Richard by Norman Richards

READING ABOUT THE PIONEERS

The American Pioneer character was an extension of the Pilgrim character. For those who were Christian it included *Faith and Steadfastness, Brotherly Love and Christian Care, Diligence and Industry,* and *Liberty of Conscience*. The principle of Voluntary Union, American Federalism, was exemplified by the Pioneer Families who helped each other as they built the communities which were to include the church and the school. Had only the saloons and the gun-shooting prevailed in our rough western communities we should never have established state after state with Biblical principles of government.

Read *Teaching and Learning,* page 40. This passage by Pastor Gregg indicates why "in taking possession of new territory we must run up the church, and we must run it up in the very beginning. The Christian Church must be there in the new territory to help formulate the character of its institutions, and to breathe the soul of Christ in all its history and in all its progress."

PIONEER MISSIONARIES — MARCUS AND NARCISSA WHITMAN:

Marcus and his wife Narcissa went to the Oregon region as missionaries in 1835. Whitman, through his work with our government was instrumental in having the Oregon country secured for the United States. Yet, on November 29, 1847 he and his wife and twelve other persons were massacred by the Indians.

One might ask what did such a mission accomplish? We know that the death of the Whitmans shocked Congress out of its indifference to the safety and protection of settlers in that territory. After the tragedy they moved to organize the territorial government of Oregon.

In the book *Narcissa Whitman, Pioneer of Oregon,* by Jeanette Eaton, Harcourt, Brace and Company, 1941, we read:

> As for the Northwest, all its historians give these pioneers a glorious place within their annals. As interest in the early days of the territory grew, settlers in their letters, speeches, and memoirs told and retold the story of what the Whitmans did for Oregon. Narcissa was the heroine of all these narratives. Men and women, who as children stopped at Waiilatpu, offered grateful thanks for an influence they never ceased to feel. Many of them had learned their letters at the Whitman school, gained skill in farming or household arts which later stood them in good stead. But the essence of that influence was not training of the mind and hand.
>
> Those who had crossed the Rocky Mountains and the blistering plains under the most primitive conditions found Narcissa Whitman an unforgettable experience. Magically in the wilderness they were welcomed at the gracious home she had created; there they shared once more civilized ways of living and something far more important. Not for her beauty nor her lovely voice was her memory most cherished; not even for the affection she shed on every child who passed through the station. The impression of her which they would never forget was how her faith brought radiance to the things of every day, exalted her love for Marcus, and at the last glorified her death.
>
> Sometimes the students of Whitman College go out to Waiilatpu — the place of rye grass — climb to the top of the hill where stands a tall, commemo-

rative shaft above the graves and there reflect upon this first pioneer woman of Oregon. Breezes from the Blue Mountains tell them what happened on that spot. Those who listen go away with hope in their hearts that this will always be the true story of America — a story of high-hearted courage and a rich humanity.

MIDWEST PIONEERS:

The series of books by Laura Ingalls Wilder deal with pioneer days in the Midwest. Beginning with *The Little House in the Big Woods* of Wisconsin, Laura Ingalls and her family traveled to Kansas in a covered wagon, to Missouri, Iowa, and Minnesota. Finally they moved from Minnesota to the Dakota territory. Six books cover the early pioneer days of the Ingalls family, with one book, *Farmer Boy,* about Almanzo Wilder who lived on a farm in northern New York state and would become Laura's husband when they met in the Dakota territory.

Mrs. Wilder's books are excellent on the Pioneer Days and provide an opportunity to study an author in depth. Her biography, *Laura* by Donald Zochert, is in paperback as are all of her delightful true stories of her own life and family.

READING ABOUT TEACHING AND LEARNING

JESSE STUART:

> *If we work upon marble, it will perish; if we work upon brass, time will efface it; if we rear temples, they will crumble into dust; but if we work upon immortal minds, if we imbue them with principles, with just fear of God and love of our fellow-men, we engrave on those tablets something which will brighten to all eternity.*
> Daniel Webster

One of the most endearing books ever written on teaching is the true autobiographical account by Jesse Stuart, *The Thread That Runs So True: The Story of a Kentucky Mountain School-Teacher.* This book has brought more young people into teaching than any other and it has re-inspired those already in the profession to new visions of what teaching can mean. As Jesse Stuart wrote in his Preface,

> As a teacher in a one-room school, where I taught all eight grades, and then high school, as a principal of rural and city high schools and superintendent of city and county school systems, I learned by experience that teaching is the greatest profession there is....
>
> I am proud that I have been a teacher and am one today. Teaching is something above and beyond teaching lessons and facts from books. It is this but more too. It is helping a youth to find a path of his own that will eventually lead him through fields of frustration and modern pitfalls of destruction until he finds himself.

It is so true that we do not live by bread alone. In any youth who has ever come to school to me I have seen something essentially good, a potential that needs to be developed. It is the teacher's duty to develop this good potential in each young individual. And teachers have done it too. Make no mistake about it. Unfortunately there is no way to measure all the good our teachers have developed in youth....

And I am firm in my belief that a teacher lives on and on through his students. I will live if my teaching is inspirational, good, and stands firm for good values and character training. Tell me how can good teaching ever die. Good teaching is forever and the teacher is immortal.

A ONE-ROOM SOUTHERN SCHOOLHOUSE
Sketch by Benson Lossing

Jesse Stuart

The Thread That Runs So True: The Story of a Kentucky Mountain School-Teacher, by Jesse Stuart,* Charles Scribner's Sons, New York, 1958.

THE STORY OF HELEN KELLER:

Of special interest to Americans is the story of Helen Keller who became blind and deaf at an early age. Through the love and the determination of a *teacher,* Annie Sullivan, Helen Keller was finally able to break through the frightening physical and emotional barriers of a dark and soundless universe. Helen Keller became a teacher and writer, endeavoring to help others to overcome impossible disadvantages. Two books can be obtained to help us appreciate this remarkable woman and her teacher, Miss Annie Sullivan.

Helen Keller by Margaret Davidson, 1969. Order from Scholastic, Inc. This is a book to read to the entire family.

Helen Keller, The Story of My Life, an autobiography. This is an Airmont Classic, but can be ordered from F.A.C.E.

READING ABOUT THE FRENCH REVOLUTION

Modern education often teaches that "the American, French, and Russian revolutions" are "links in a single historical chain." But this is totally false.

In 1800 John Quincy Adams, our sixth President to be, translated a work by Friedrich Gentz in which he compared the French and American revolutions. Adams was concerned lest the Americans of his day confuse the principles of the two revolutions. Stefan T. Possony of the Hoover Institution added his *Reflections on the Russian Revolution* to complete the comparison. Published in 1959 by Henry Regnery Company of Chicago [OP], this little paperback is invaluable to set the record straight. As Possony concludes:

> To summarize the contrasts, the American revolution was begotten in freedom and ended in order. It created a stable state and a stable society in which

the vital forces of the nation could be used for the betterment of itself and of all mankind.

The French revolution began as an attempt at orderly reform of monarchy, degenerated from freedom into anarchy, and from there it was reversed into dictatorship and eventual restoration....

The Russian revolution, which promised a classless society, and the elimination of tyranny and ultimately of the state itself, was the most ambitious of these three revolutions. It was begotten in disorder and it led to greater disorder....

The French revolution cost much and achieved little. The American revolution cost little and achieved much; it was a successful *liberating* revolution. The Russian revolution cost enormously and proved to be the most thoroughly *enslaving* revolution of history. To paraphrase Lenin, the American revolution was one step forward, the Russian revolution was many steps backward. "By their fruits, ye shall know them."

Three Revolutions: The French and American Revolutions compared by Friedrich Gentz; Reflections on the Russian Revolution by Stefan T. Possony, Gateway Edition 6023, Henry Regnery Company, 1959 [OP].

TWO NOVELS ON THE FRENCH REVOLUTION:

There are two outstanding novels with the French Revolution as backdrop. These are written by English authors. The first is *The Scarlet Pimpernell* by the Baroness Orczy, available in paperback from Airmont Classics. This is the thrilling story of the elusive Englishman known but unknown as *the Scarlet Pimpernell.* The little red countryside flower was the identification of a courageous group of men who risked their lives in helping doomed French aristocrats escape from the Reign of Terror and the insatiable appetite of Madame La Guillotine.

The second novel, by the imcomparable Charles Dickens, is *A Tale of Two Cities.** This is one of the great novels of the world and its theme is not only revolution — but redemption also. Mr. Dickens works with a large number of characters and with a big canvas — but he is a master artist at the development of character as well as of setting and of plot. It provides the reader with a good look at the excesses of Godless revolution where liberty with law is replaced by anarchy and license.

THE TAKING OF THE BASTILLE

"Americans can be grateful that we are beneficiaries of the only Christian revolution in history — a return to base, a return to Biblical principles of character and government." (*The Christian History of the American Revolution: Consider and Ponder* compiled and edited by Verna M. Hall.)

READING SOME OF OUR KEY AUTHORS IN DEPTH

The Christian History Literature Program beginning at Kindergarten and including Literature Courses in College, endeavors to restore to homes and schools those Key Authors, who in their writings identify the character of nations on the Chain of Christianity.

First, because of the English Bible, the Textbook of Liberty, we find English writers who brought forth the character of their own land as it was affected by Christianity. Then, in America, as Christianity moved Westward with individual liberty under law, we find our first American writers giving the world the character of liberty.

Most of these authors need to be read carefully and they are taught in our Principle Approach schools. But it is fine for families to introduce them in the Family Reading Aloud, for, then they become authors loved by the whole family. We shall mention just a few of these Key Authors whom you can begin to explore.

CHARLES DICKENS

Charles Dickens was born in the midst of the Industrial Revolution in England which created a world of opportunity and a world of difficult living conditions. Because of a decline in Christianity there was often little consistency between the church-going capitalist and the working conditions under which he permitted his employees to exist. But Dickens believed that poverty, and abominable tenements could be eliminated if industrialists and property owners would only practice their Christianity in the market place.

Charles Dickens believed in social reform but he believed that the key to social reform lay in the reformation of character. His novels are dictionaries of the English character of the nineteenth century. And he displays an innumerable company of men, women, and especially of children whom we come to know and love or despise. Dickens' settings give us a picture of those conditions of poverty which need reform. Above all he gives us a picture of the human spirit which overcomes the world of hopelessness, poverty, and hatred.

Dickens was the most widely read author in England and America. When he died in 1870 he left a literary legacy never to be forgotten. His characters have become immortalized. Here are a few titles to begin with:

THE CRATCHIT FAMILY CHRISTMAS

Christmas Books. This collection of shorter stories introduce you and your family to Dickens' great gift to the middle and lower classes — the celebration of Christmas. For the rich the enjoyment of festivity was perpetual but for those who had to work every day of the year — except Christmas — the joy of the Christmas festival was restored in these stories. Above all read our perennial *A Christmas Carol* and other stories like *A Cricket on the Hearth* and *The Chimes*. The main characters are poor people who find joy in simple pleasures. These are stories to read every year at Christmas time — out loud to family and friends.

Eleanor Farjeon, English author in her own right, in the Introduction to the Centennial Edition of Dickens' Works describes the *Christmas Books* as follows:

> Warm humanity pervades the Dickens Christmas, in it the paramount needs are those of the Child; he had always with him the Poor, whose poverty was not God's divine example, but man's crying shame. And he cried it, how he cried it, from the housetops! — the wealth of Dives jostling the want of Lazarus, Trotty Veck's humble dish of tripe made humbler by Sir Joseph Bowley's opulent cheque-book; above all, Scrooge, who, obliged to subscribe to the prisons and the Poor Law, shut his eyes to the conditions of those ghastly institutions, which were then Society's answer to want and ignorance: until the Spirit which came to haunt him produced from its robe two children. "Oh, Man! look here!"
>
> ...Small wonder we grew up adoring the name of Dickens and devouring his works. As for the Dickens Christmas, the little Farjeons knew all about that; their father saw to it that no household had a more Dickensian Christmas than his. A Christmas long remembered, not only by his children, but by the scores of young and old who experienced his hospitality at this season, a Christmas in which jollity, liberality, and charity were sisters. And in our home, as in the Christmas Books to which the English poor owed an unrepayable debt, the greatest of these was Charity.

Other Dickens Books:

The Personal History of David Copperfield was always Dickens' own favorite book, perhaps because it was autobiographical of his own life. Especially the first fourteen chapters, there are sixty-four in all, represent an excellent introduction to the younger life of David Copperfield. (It is out of print except in collections.)

by Jessie Willcox Smith

Great Expectations* is another favorite of Dickens' books. It starts very dramatically and includes many interesting characters — but in the end the hero's character has improved, he has become humbler, and the heroine has been released from the unnatural character put upon her — and all ends well.

A Tale of Two Cities* is the most dramatic of Dickens' novels as we have already indicated with its background of the French Revolution.

In the 35 years of his productive writing Charles Dickens composed 15 novels, several plays, innumerable short stories, and a host of miscellaneous articles in his two weeklies, *Household Words* and *All the Year Round*. You will have to choose which other novels of Dickens you would like to read — after you have read the above.

To study the author there is a delightful book written for younger readers entitled, *Introducing Charles Dickens* by May Lamberton Becker, 1940, Dodd, Mead.

For the student who wishes to study Dickens in depth and who would enjoy a summary of each major work, read *Charles Dickens: His Tragedy and Triumph,* by Edgar Johnson, 1952, Simon & Schuster.

CHARLES DICKENS AND HIS SAVIOUR JESUS CHRIST

One Dickens book, *The Life of Our Lord,* written for his children during the years 1846–49, and not published until 1934, was withheld from the reading public. In his own words he stated:

> I have always striven in my writings to express veneration for the life and lessons of Our Saviour, because I feel it; and because I rewrote that history for my children — everyone of whom knew it from having it repeated to them — long before they could read, and almost as soon as they could speak. But I have never made proclamation of this from the housetops.

Dickens feared that "a public disclosure of so intimate a document might involve the possibility of attack and defense of his deepest religious convictions."

In his day Dickens, as his writings reveal, felt concerned that those who professed the most Christianity within the church, did not practice it outside the church — in the market place of daily life. The spirit of Christianity and its impact upon the world of love, of forgiveness, and of doing right, most touched his heart. This is what he wrote in the last paragraph of the book, after the ascension of our Lord, and the persecution of His disciples as they endeavored to preach the Gospel:

> Remember! — It is Christianity TO DO GOOD, always — even to those who do evil to us. It is Christianity to love our neighbors as ourself, and to do to all men as we would have them do to us. It is Christianity to be gentle, merciful, and forgiving, and to keep those qualities quiet in our own hearts, and never make a boast of them, or of our prayers or of our love of God, but always to show that we love Him by humbly trying to do right in everything. If we do this, and remember the life and lessons of Our Lord Jesus Christ, and try to act up to them, we may confidently hope that God will forgive us our sins and mistakes, and enable us to live and die in peace.

SIR WALTER SCOTT

Sir Walter Scott endeared himself to countless readers in both England and America with his historical novels. It is only in the past fifty years that we have stopped reading Scott in our schools. Scott exemplified the purpose of literature — to teach us:

> *Who* we are as a nation
> *Where* our principles and ideals come from — their sources
> *What* our purpose is as a nation

This is also the major purpose of writers in every land — especially those lands where the Chain of Christianity has helped bring forth a history of liberty. Sir Walter Scott did this first for his own nation, Scotland. Edgar Johnson in his exhaustive twelve-year study of Scott, writes in his Introduction to his two-volume *Sir Walter Scott, the Great Unknown,* Macmillan, 1970:

No Scottish name is more widely known than that of Walter Scott. With Robert Bruce, with Robert Burns, with Mary Queen of Scots, it is among those that have echoed throughout the world. His country's name and fame, her bloody and heroic past, Scott celebrated to mankind. All save one of his major poems, twenty-two of his thirty-two works of prose fiction, have their scene in his native land and are filled with Scottish song and story, Scottish lakes and mountains and glens, Scottish men and women. Appropriately, he who gave such luster to Scotland, derives his very name from the land he loved.

But Scott did more than just bring to life the song and story and character and history of his native land — he accomplished the same thing with all periods of history which his pen and genius touched...Scott threw down the gauntlet to those who believed that history was "as dry as dust" and his success transformed the past into life through the vitality of his characters and his dramatic presentation of historical events.

SCOTT'S CONTRIBUTIONS TO LITERATURE ON THE CHAIN OF CHRISTIANITY

Scott created the historical novel. He revitalized history as a source for dramatic fiction through poetry and verse.

Scott identified history and literature as the mirror of the character of a nation or a people.

Scotland discovered her own individuality through the writings of Sir Walter Scott.

Scott identified Christianity as a main force in history, character, and government, and revealed these in his writings.

Most of Scott's novels have Christian themes and illustrate Biblical principles. Scott, unlike most writers of today, was a moralist. He was concerned with character — the struggle for what is right and determination to oppose the elements of evil wherever found.

Scott set a standard for a vitality and a quality of historical writing that influenced other writers including American James Fenimore Cooper and Frenchman Alexandre Dumas. Scott's individual character and friendship helped many other writers. Washington Irving, whose own background was of Scottish origin, loved Scott dearly and found warmth of approval and personal help from the more mature author.

*Ivanhoe*** is Scott's most famous historical novel. It has its setting during the Anglo-Saxon and Norman period when the Saxon was fighting to retain his independence and his capacity for self-government.

Quentin Durwood, set against a vivid background of 15th century France, and the court of Louis XI, and the political ambitions of Charles, Duke of Burgandy, once again pits character, courage, and bravery against intrigue and violence. In the end our hero wins fair lady, wealth, rank, and prominence. The end of feudalism and chivalry is not the end of Christian character — but rather its liberation.

The Talisman is set in the Third Crusade with Richard of England, but its main characters are Saladin, Moslem Knight, and Sir Kenneth, Scottish Knight. Scott again challenges the romantic irrationality of the Crusades, the inconsistency of Chivalry, and the importance of Christianity as the measure of a man — Christian or non-Christian. *The Talisman* is relevant reading for today and should be abridged and reprinted.

BIOGRAPHY OF SIR WALTER SCOTT:

For a delightful biography, the following book written for junior high provides adults and young people with an excellent character study of Scott: *Sir Walter Scott: Wizard of the North* by Pearle Henriksen Schultz,** Vanguard Press, 1967, (with photographs).

Highlights of the Book

The Character of the Boy: "With a courage that is heart high" (p. 46).

The Character of the Young Man: "We each carry our own heart's burden" (p. 72).

The Character of the Man: "This is my own, my native land" (p. 95). Scott taught his children their own history around the family fire.

Scott's Style of Research and Writing:

"He jotted a little reminder in the notebook that seldom left his hand on trips like these" (p. 111).

Scott's Response to Success:

"Scott became famous at the age of thirty-three with the publication of *The Lay of the Last Minstrel*. Nothing in the history of publishing had been quite like the frantic demand for this poem." (p. 102)

Scott refused the offer to make him poet laureate of Great Britain (p. 115).

Scott's dream of Abbotsford (p. 119).

Scott's Responsibility to His Nation:

Scott restored to his nation through history and poetry their native character, and through the Prince Regent, permission to restore Scotland's Royal Regalia.

Scott's Response to Affliction:

"Out of his personal tragedies he built a life of noble courage" (p. 195); to illness and pain (p. 20; 64–70; 149–150); to his debt of honor (p. 183).

Before you read or teach a Scott novel, study a good map of Scotland and find a good travel book on Scotland.

READING WASHINGTON IRVING IN DEPTH

Washington Irving (1783–1859) was our first man of letters in the American Republic after the establishment of our Constitution, allowing greater individual liberty and productivity. Named for our first President, Irving, a resident of New York City, where the first capital of our country was established, early evidenced an interest in writing about America. His very first book of note was *Knickerbocker's History of New York*. Diedrich

Knickerbocker was the imaginary Dutch historian which Irving created in order that he might write a humorous history of New York "From the beginning of the World to the End of the Dutch Dynasty."

For such a young man to write such an amusing satire of New York under three of her Dutch Governors was an accomplishment. And it stamped the word "Knickerbocker" upon the city.

> I find its very name become a "household word" and used to give the home stamp to everything recommended for popular acceptation, such as Knickerbocker societies, Knickerbocker insurance companies, Knickerbocker steamboats, Knickerbocker omnibuses, Knickerbocker bread, and Knickerbocker ice — and when I find New Yorkers of Dutch descent priding themselves upon being "genuine Knickerbocker" — I please myself with the persuasion that I have struck the right chord; that my dealings with the good old Dutch times, and the customs and usages derived from them, are in harmony with the feelings and humors of my townsmen...

Readers on both sides of the Atlantic enjoyed Washington Irving's humorous book — especially Sir Walter Scott who read it aloud around the fireside and praised it publicly.

Irving's next book was *The Sketch-Book of Geoffrey Crayon, Gentleman.** These sketches of English and American national character, portrayed gently, were a publishing sensation, once again, in both America and England. These sketches or essays, and short stories, are among the most delightful in the English language.

Washington Irving's serious work dealing with American history and character began with his first sojourn in Spain in a post of the American legation with his friend, Alexander Everett, American Minister to Madrid. Here Irving discovered the original manuscripts concerning Columbus. He wrote *Life of Columbus* in 1828, and launched an American biography about the efforts of the first man to make the Atlantic crossing westward. In addition Washington Irving also discovered Spanish history. In fact, today Spain celebrates the writings of Washington Irving as one who describes its past history and provides travelers with a guide to its Moorish buildings.

Of all our American writers, Washington Irving's writings follow a consecutive path of our history — especially from its pre-existence through Columbus' discoveries — and including his five-volume biography of the Father of our Country, George Washington.

When the Steamboat opened up travel by our rivers Irving was enabled to go west and to make *A Tour on the Prairies* and to see the frontier which was drawing so many thousands of pioneers. He hunted the vanishing buffalo, met the Indian, and sensed the vastness and loneliness of the prairie.

Washington Irving's major volume on the west was *Astoria,* or the account of the two expeditions organized in 1810 by John Jacob Astor — one by land, one by sea, to the mouth of the Columbia River where he hoped to establish the capital of a vast fur-trading empire. This book and his *The Adventures of Captain Bonneville, U.S.A.* in the Rocky Mountains and the Far West, have both been republished by the University of Oklahoma

Press, and represent a valuable contribution to our knowledge of the brave men who forged our paths westward.

What to Read of Washington Irving

Every family would enjoy Reading Aloud the two choice stories which Irving wrote about the Dutch settlers in the Hudson River valley: *Rip Van Winkle and The Legend of Sleepy Hollow* by Washington Irving, illustrated by Fritz Kredel, has been published in a big handsome book by Sleepy Hollow Restorations. It can be purchased for $10 or more, but it is a valuable and enjoyable introduction to one of America's most important authors. (If you do not care for the style of these illustrations, there are many other editions in your library.)

SLEEPY HOLLOW CREEK

The Sketch Book* in its entirety can be purchased in paperback, Signet Classic CE1263. A collection from several sources in paperback by Irving, *The Legend of Sleepy Hollow and Other Stories,** can be purchased from Airmont Classics (CL 150).

The two most important writings of Irving for every American after the short stories and essays above, are the biographies of *Columbus* and *George Washington*. You will have to look for these in your own public library — or in the old book stores. Irving's *Life of Washington* is still the finest literary biography of our first President and one which will be a treasure to read within your family circle.

Washington Irving lived near Tarrytown in a home which he created on the Hudson River which he named *Sunnyside*. This home can still be visited and it is the center of *Sleepy Hollow Restorations* built around the life and times and writings of Washington Irving.

There are some extensive biographies of Irving. Professor Stanley T. Williams of Yale University published through Oxford University Press a two-volume study in 1935. Yet, we still prefer the writings of the individual author himself as a first introduction to his life and to his convictions. *Life and Letters of Washington Irving* by his nephew, Pierre M. Irving, is one of the best sources to Irving. Here is to be found his own account of many events of his life and of his work on the books he published.

"SUNNYSIDE," THE RESIDENCE OF WASHINGTON IRVING
Sketches by Benson Lossing

Washington Irving Goes Home

Brought up by a strictly religious father, Irving did not join the church until late in life. Yet, he was a man of religious principles and of Christian ideals. After the loss of his childhood sweetheart, Irving never married; but he was essentially a family man and surrounded himself with the happy homes of nephews and nieces who were married.

Sunnyside was indeed a joyous gathering place.

Washington Irving considered his biography of George Washington, undertaken at the end of his life, as "my crowning labor." As his nephew, Pierre Irving, editor and associate, wrote at his passing,

> I could not but remember his last words to me, more than a year ago, when his book was finished, and his health was failing: "I am getting ready to go; I am shutting up my doors and windows." And I could not but feel that they were all open now, and bright with the light of eternal morning.

Tales of the Alhambra, Irving's most celebrated account of the huge old Arabic palaces of Granada, Spain, has been republished in different editions. One of the most recent, a 1979 republication with photographs in color, is by Crescent Books, a Division of Crown Publishers, Inc., now through Random House, Inc.

Irving spent a number of weeks living in the Alhambra in 1829 and he had this to say of his experiences:

> Here, then, I am nestled in one of the most remarkable, romantic, and delicious spots in the world. . . . I breakfast in the saloon of the ambassadors, or among the flowers and fountains in the court of the Lions, and when I am not occupied with my pen, I lounge with my books about these oriental apartments, or stroll about the courts, and gardens, and arcades, by day or night, with no one to interrupt me. It absolutely appears to me like a dream; or as if I am spell-bound in some fairy palace. . . . I have nothing but the sound of water, the humming of bees, and the singing of nightingales to interrupt the profound silence of my abode. . . .

READING NATHANIEL HAWTHORNE IN DEPTH

Nathaniel Hawthorne (1804–1864) emerged from his New England background as a powerful American writer. While he struggled for recognition as all America had to do, Hawthorne married Sophia Peabody and enjoyed family life and his children. His standards for writing for the young are most heartening and represent a position that seems to have been overlooked by many contemporary writers.

> The author regards children as sacred, and would not for the world, cast anything into the fountain of a young heart, that might embitter and pollute its waters. And, even in point of the reputation to be aimed at, juvenile literature is as well worth cultivating as any other. The writer, if he succeed in pleasing his little readers, may hope to be remembered by them till their own old age — a far longer period of literary existence than is generally attained, by those who seek immortality from the judgments of full grown men.

In 1851 Hawthorne brought out *A Wonder Book** which presented the classical myths in a delightful form, suitable for children's reading. Here are to be found some of the immortal old tales in a moral setting: King Midas whose Golden Touch extended even unto his little daughter; Pandora's Box — opened by her curiosity; Old Philemon and his wife, Baucis, who in their charity "entertained strangers unawares" and were forever represented as intertwined trees, an oak and a linden-tree, where "the weary, and the hungry, and the thirsty used to repose themselves, and quaff milk abundantly out of the miraculous pitcher."

Hawthorne followed *A Wonder Book** with a similar volume, *Tanglewood Tales*. Included were the famed *Minotaur, The Dragon's Teeth, Circe's Palace, The Golden Fleece* and others.

The Scarlet Letter* is Hawthorne's most famous novel — a novel of sin and its uncovering which is faithfully taught in most Christian schools and colleges. It is however a fearful reminder of some of the harsher moments of Puritan New England.

The House of Seven Gables* was preferred by Hawthorne to his masterpiece. In this novel, which has some touches of gloom in a family curse, there is however opportunity for love to be of a quality that can dispel hatred and become part of the setting for retribution and forgiveness.

Salem, Massachusetts is the location of the real old House of Seven Gables, with its secret passage, through which visitors are conducted upstairs. In this novel, Hawthorne portrays his wife through *Phoebe* whose warmth, sunshine, and domesticity bring great charm to transform what might be a tale of doom and gloom into a love story.

Perhaps the most interesting of Nathaniel Hawthorne's books written especially for his own children is his *Grandfather's Chair: True Stories from New England History and Biography* [OP]. Like Sir Walter Scott's *Tales of a Grandfather, Being Stories from the History of Scotland,* and Charles Dickens' *A Child's History of England,* this is an excellent effort to introduce the very young to their own history.

Hawthorne used the literary device of an Old Chair which had been brought to America aboard the ship *Arabella,* that ship which brought Lady Arbella and Governor Winthrop and the first Puritans to New England. As the chair was passed along from one colonist to another the history of New England was being made. Many illustrious characters are introduced to the children: Roger Williams, John Eliot and the first American Bible, Cotton Mather and witches, and many important events of Colonial and Revolutionary history. It is all in small bites and related by Grandfather to his Grandchildren as he sits in the chair and they gather around him.

Grandfather's Chair can be found in many libraries and even in some of the old bookstores. What a delightful way to introduce your children to our own history — and to illustrate it by discussion and perhaps a trip to New England — after you are well prepared to "see" what you have already learned of America's Christian History and Biography.

Today it is possible to purchase in paperback from Airmont Classics, six of Hawthorne's works; among these are *The House of the Seven Gables,* The Scarlet Letter,* A Wonder Book,** and *Tanglewood Tales*. There are countless biographies of Hawthorne, yet nothing can surpass the letters and diaries written by the author himself about himself, to really help us to know this major writer of American character in New England.

RESTORING HEROES AND HEROINES TO OUR READING ALOUD

In his study of heroes through history Thomas Carlyle (1795–1881) wrote:

> For, as I take it, Universal History, the history of what man has accomplished in this world, is at bottom the History of the Great Men who have worked here. ...
>
> One comfort is, that Great Men, taken up in any way, are profitable company. We cannot look, however imperfectly, upon a great man, without gaining something by him. He is the living light-fountain, which it is good and pleasant to be near... a natural luminary shining by the gift of Heaven....
>
> Look now... at that little Fact of the sailing of the Mayflower, two hundred years ago, from Delft Haven in Holland!... For it was properly the beginning of America: there were straggling settlers in America before, some material as of a body was there; but the soul of it was this. These poor men, first driven out of their country, not able well to live in Holland, determine on settling in the New World....
>
> In Neal's *History of the Puritans* is an account of the ceremony of their departure: solemnity, we might call it rather, for it was a real act of worship. Their minister went down with them to the beach, and their brethren whom they were to leave behind; all joined in solemn prayer, That God would have pity on His poor children, and *go* with them into that waste wilderness, for He also had made that, He was there also as well as here. — Hah! These men, I think, had a work! The weak thing, weaker than a child, becomes strong one day, if it be a true thing. (*On Heroes, Hero-Worship and the Heroic in History,* 1838; University of Nebraska Press, 1966)

As Carlyle himself stated, *heroes* have gone out of fashion — and our age, too, "denies the desirableness of great men." And, since we will consider the need for a generation of Great Men and Great Women, we, too, must state with Carlyle that: "No sadder proof can be given by a man of his own littleness than disbelief in great men."

To bring forth greatness in America we must once again begin to believe in men and women who can act in accord with Christ for the needs of the times. We can have as many heroes and heroines as we have American Christians who will commit themselves for both Christ and country — the restoration of this country which He gave us — through other Great Men and Women. Indeed, we need Great Men, Women, and Children who will be not the "creatures" of our age, but the "creators" of it — of a better age than we have had under the unrighteous.

From the time of the Pilgrims and before, we have had brave men and women who have helped shape and form our nation under God's direction. We have had heroes who have died in the faith. But our interest in this program of restoration of Reading Aloud in the home, is to restore to our own minds and hearts the knowledge of some who have lived in our history — both past and present — and who are an encouragement and often an example to our own efforts. Noah Webster speaks of the *Heroic* as pertaining to "Brave; intrepid; magnanimous; enterprising; illustrious for valor...." We think in this century of men conquering some of our last outposts — the seventh continent, *Antarctica* and *space.*

Particularly in the early part of our century, individual effort was notable in the conquest of Antarctica. One of the first men to venture forth in this area was Richard E. Byrd.

Arnold Guyot, America's first Professor of Christian Geography, wrote in his *Physical Geography,* 1873:

> The EARTH, as the subject of geographical science, may be regarded in two different points of view: —
>
> 1. In ITSELF, as a master-piece of Divine workmanship, perfect in all its parts and conditions.
>
> 2. In ITS PURPOSE, as the abode of Man, the scene of his activity, and the means of his development.
>
> The first gives rise to the *Geography of Nature,* and the second to the *Geography of Man.*

In the study of the six continents for man's abode, Guyot designated the three Northern Continents as *"The Continents of History"* and the Southern Continents as *"The Continents of Nature."* He qualified his designations as follows, from page 149 of *Teaching and Learning America's Christian History: The Principle Approach:*

> *The Southern Continents...* where all the conditions that stimulate physical life are the most powerful... man has remained at the bottom of the social scale.
> *The Northern Continents...* they possess all the conditions most favorable for the development and progress of the races inhabiting them.

The *seventh continent* seems to have none of the qualifications of either the northern or southern continents. It is true that the physical conditions are all-powerful — but they do not support growth of living plant, animal, or vegetable life — except perhaps some lichens or mosses which grow on exposed rock. In short, it would seem that God did not intend that *Antarctica* should be inhabited, for all conditions favorable for man are absent.

But the vastness of this southern continent, at the bottom of the earth, and its importance to the study of weather, and perhaps as a possible polar route for air flight from down-under to America, represented the most overwhelming challenge of any place on the planet.

HERO OF ANTARCTICA: ADMIRAL RICHARD E. BYRD

In 1929, Admiral Byrd was the first American to drop our flag on the geographical point known as 90° South — the South Pole — the axis of the earth. This was the climax of a century of acquaintance with the existence of Antarctica and efforts to conquer it. Captain James Cook crossed the Antarctic Circle in 1773, the first man to do so, typical of that intrepid explorer and navigator.

While men had gone before him, men like the brave Englishman Captain Falcon Scott, who with his four companions met death in 1912, on their return trip from their trek to the pole, it was Byrd who introduced the technology of the 20th century to the last continent.

The efforts for mere survival in winter temperatures below minus 100 degrees Fahrenheit required man to bring in all the help of machines and scientific instrumentation that was being produced. The 1957–8 International Geophysical Year represented the most concerted attack by men of 66 nations on Antarctica.

ADMIRAL RICHARD E. BYRD

But before this massive effort by nations, Richard Evelyn Byrd was one of the lonely pioneers in the exploration of Antarctica. His four expeditions in 1928, 1933, 1939, and 1947 were efforts which revealed his character under conditions of stress in the discovered parts of the world as he sought to raise funds for his ventures.

Admiral Byrd's bravery and valor were also demonstrated in the dramatic five months which he spent *alone* — in *complete solitude* at a weather station some 100 miles south of the camp at Little America. Here Byrd battled with death. He was determined not to call for help because he did not wish to endanger other men's lives in their efforts to rescue him. His account in his book *Alone* is one of the great accounts of the heroism of the twentieth century. He was alone with God.

Admiral Byrd described the turning point in his critical survival in Antarctica:

> Few men during their lifetime come anywhere near exhausting the resources dwelling within them. There are deep wells of strength that are never used. Could I find a way to tap those physical potentialities locked up within myself? Well, suppose I were able to. It still wouldn't mean a great deal. Clearly, my remaining material resources couldn't be very much. Therefore I must find other sources of replenishment. In such times, when the tricks and expediencies of cornered men fall to pieces in their hands, they turn to God — as I did, after my fashion. (*Alone* by Richard E. Byrd, 1938, Avon Books, NY, p. 144)

RESOURCES:

Admiral Richard E. Byrd by Alfred Steinberg, from *The Lives to Remember* Series, published by G. P. Putnam's Sons, 1960. This is an excellent youthful biography.

Alone by Richard E. Byrd, G. P. Putnam's Sons, 1938.

Other books by Richard Evelyn Byrd are *Little America* and *Skyward* which you can find at the library or in an old bookstore, and *Discovery* available from Ayer.

It is significant that Americans have played such an important role in the efforts to conquer this vast continent of ice — the highest and coldest of all continents sitting at an average of 6,000 feet and rising to 10,000 in its mountains. But America with its own unique Christian history and Biblical form of government, made up of all nations and races, has been able to launch the combined efforts of many nations to work together scientifically for the improvement of the planet.

In 1860, in a personal appeal to the civilized nations of his day, Commander Matthew Fontaine Maury, Christian founder of modern oceanography, wrote:

> If, in pleading the cause of Antarctic exploration, I be required to answer first the question of *cui bono?* which is so apt to be put, I reply, it is enough for me, when contemplating the vast extent of that unknown region, to know that it is part of the surface of our planet, and to remember that *the earth was made for man;* that all knowledge is profitable; that no discoveries have conferred more honour and glory upon the age in which they were made, or been more beneficial to the world, than geographical discoveries; and that never were nations so well prepared to undertake Antarctic exploration as those that I now solicit.

It was almost one hundred years later that the nations of the world turned their attention to Antarctica — so occupied had they been with other projects of mutual concern — including war.

The Crossing of Antarctica: The Commonwealth Trans-Antarctic Expedition 1955–1958 by Sir Vivian Fuchs and Sir Edmund Hillary, Little Brown and Company, 1959. A double effort from both sides of the continent. The last 2500 miles of uncrossed territory with "faith and science."

Antarctica by Emil Schulthess, Simon and Schuster, N.Y. 1960. A textual and photographic account of 1956/57 Operation Deep Freeze IV, part of the International Geophysical Year. A large-sized book rich in its contributions to our knowledge and understanding of Antarctica — for the layman. Schulthess catches "the fairyland grandeur of glaciers and icebergs — the awesome spectacle of yawning caverns and crevasses that moaned as the ice shelf moved relentlessly toward the sea at the rate of four feet a day. He caught, too, the changing moods of men at work and play" and the Weddell seals and Emperor Penguins — the few creatures which exist in the seas around the edge of the continent.

See also "Special Research Expedition, Antarctica, God's Seventh Continent: 'Seeking the Biblical Purpose of God's Seventh Continent,' 'Inspiring Teachers to Study Antarctica,' and 'Teaching Elementary Students Admiral Byrd's *Alone:* an Armchair Odyssey to Antarctica'," found in Volume One of *The Journal of the Foundation for American Christian Education,* San Francisco, 1989.

CHARLES A. LINDBERGH: HERO OF MODERN AVIATION

The twentieth century is the century of fast transportation — first *wheels* — then *wings* — first cars or automobiles — then planes. One of the first heroes of this *age of flight* was Charles Augustus Lindbergh.

Born of talented parents in Minnesota, Charles Lindbergh left his engineering courses at the University of Wisconsin during his second year to go into flying. His father, a United States Congressman, was "dead set against the idea. He said, 'Flying is too dangerous and you're my only son.' He offered him a choice of careers in business or farming.... But in the end C. A. Lindbergh capitulated and later even helped the boy borrow some money at the bank to buy his first airplane." (Walter S. Ross, *The Last Hero: Charles A. Lindbergh,* Harper and Row, New York, 1964, p. 43)

Lindbergh's mother was concerned but said, "All right. If you really want to fly, that's what you should do." Mrs. C. A. Lindbergh — Evelyn Lodge Land — "at a time when few women got any kind of higher education, took a Bachelor of Science degree at the University of Michigan and then went on to get her Master's degree in science at Columbia University in New York. Her education was enough to set her apart from other women, and she was not merely intellectual but attractive as well. She came of a family with deep roots in North America." (Ross, p. 27)

Like so many of the men who learned to fly during the beginning of commercial aviation, Lindbergh's experience included "barnstorming" or exhibition flying. These tours around the country were to introduce the public to aviation — unfortunately associating it with thrills and daredevil stunts. Lindbergh's mother, always a source of strength and encouragement, became a flying enthusiast when her son took her "on a ten-day barnstorming tour. Later in his career, when he became an air-mail pilot, she would often ride with him, sitting on the mail sacks in the front cockpit." (Ross, p. 57)

Lindbergh joined the Army Air Corps because he learned that they trained pilots and because he believed he would get experience with a number of types of planes. He graduated at the top of his class with the rank of Second Lieutenant in the Army Air Service Reserve. At twenty-three years of age he was a veteran pilot.

Lindbergh's preparation for what was to become the "flight of the century" included training other pilots, more barnstorming, and finally, flying the U.S. Mail on the first airmail service. Only those men who experienced the early days of individual daring in all kinds of planes and in all kinds of weather could convey to us what has now become commonplace in mail service. Even in the days when few letters filled the mail sacks Lindbergh, who had from the first days of flight envisioned its wonder and its possibilities to liberate man — began to dream of "a nonstop" flight from New York to Paris.

Today, as we look back over the short distance of time between Lindbergh's New York-to-Paris idea and its realization, it seems incredible. Actually, in 1926 there were a number of efforts in the making to put some well-known aviator, like Richard E. Byrd, into a reputable plane and make the trans-Atlantic flight. Young Lindbergh at twenty-four would not even have been considered in such a proposal. But it was his own initiative to take all of the steps to bring his dream into reality. It is a tribute to his character and competence and his care to investigate every aspect that this young determined American had by February of 1927 — three months before his actual flight — secured the backing of a group of business men in St. Louis and negotiated with Ryan Airlines factory in San Diego to build a plane including his specifications and assistance. They agreed to do it — in two months time — and Lindbergh was to fly it — one pilot in a monoplane — a single engine ship. "The airplane was going to be designed and built around Lindbergh and nobody else. This would take a bit more time than adapting a tested design, but had the advantage of creating a ship just for Lindbergh's purpose.... On April 28, 1927, the *Spirit of St. Louis* was finished... the most beautiful airplane Lindbergh had ever seen." (Ross, pp. 89, 93)

When Charles A. Lindbergh began his few days of testing his new plane at Dutch Flats, near San Diego, he was tabulating the score of flights already attempted that year. Every one of the big multi-engine planes built for the New York-to-Paris flight had crashed.

Four men had lost their lives and three others had been injured. It had been his contention that the flight should be made in a single-engine plane. Even now he was under the pressure of other men, men like Byrd, readying their efforts to take off any day. It would seem that God was making the selection of who was to take this most perilous flight of the century.

The words of Charles Lindbergh alone can begin to convey to us why such a man had been chosen for such a time and such an event as this. From his own American classic, *The Spirit of St. Louis,* he wrote:

> This morning I'm going to test the *Spirit of St. Louis*. It's the 28th of April — just over two months since I placed our order with the Ryan Company, and exactly sixty days since business formalities were completed and work on the plane began. What a beautiful machine it is resting there on the field in front of the hangar, trim and slender, gleaming in its silver coat! All our ideas, all our calculations, all our hopes lie there before me, waiting to undergo the acid test of flight. For me, it seems to contain the whole future of aviation. When such planes can be built, there's no limitation to the air. In a few minutes I'll make the first take-off — for I plan to run all tests myself. (Charles A. Lindbergh, *The Spirit of St. Louis,* Macmillan, 1953, p. 120)

On May 10th, Lindbergh took off for his flight across the continent — first to St. Louis and his backers — then on to New York. Choosing to fly by night to give himself further night-time experience, he left in the late afternoon. Fourteen hours later he touched down in St. Louis, having set a record — no man ever traveled so fast from the Pacific coast before. The next morning he took off for New York — and his rendezvous with his individual place in Providence.

It was during the few days preceding his historic flight that Charles Lindbergh began to experience the invasion of the press and the publicity which came to such tragic consequences in his later life. Even his mother, disturbed by the stories in the newspapers came to spend one day with him. She wanted to talk to her son "to make sure I really wanted to go and felt it was the right thing to do. Then, she said, she would return home. She had never meant to stay, because she knew that would take my attention from the flight." (Lindbergh, p. 164)

We can imagine how Mrs. Evelyn Lindbergh felt during that tense thirty-four hours when, teaching her classes in Detroit, her heart was filled with prayer and hope for her son — America's Lone Eagle — as he flew his small monoplane sometimes at ten feet over the thousands of ocean miles towards the continent of Europe.

Lindbergh devotes almost 300 of his 500 pages of *The Spirit of St. Louis* to details of the flight as he reconstructed them. And, he weaves throughout the book, during the long hours and flight-logging, large sections on his life up to this time. This is a book which particularly belongs to the heart and mind of every American of the twentieth century. It is a book which can be reread a number of times and should be — so that we can appreciate what kind of courage, of attention to detail, of planning and preparation was required to bring this man to a readiness for his pioneer flight — a flight which launched commercial aviation in our century.

In this latter part of the twentieth century we have lost much of our wonder and excitement. So many great events have filled this century, and perhaps the individual hero has almost disappeared. Scientific achievements which are given great attention seem to be more collective than individual. That is why the careful and suspenseful reading of Lindbergh's own account can help us re-create the triumph of that first trans-ocean flight in 1927.

Tens of thousands of people and cars jammed Parisian highways as the three sightings of Lindbergh's plane — over Ireland, over Plymouth, England, and over Cherbourg — had alerted them to the arrival of the *Spirit of St. Louis*. As the tired, dazed young American of twenty-five years tried to jump out of his small plane hands reached up and lifted him out as if he were a baby. In a minute more thousands had broken through the barriers and indeed, Lindbergh could hear the sound of tearing fabric as souvenir hunters began their ravages. It was necessary to mount a guard around this fragile representation of the spirit of a new age. It was May 22, 1927 and it will forever be an historic moment — in the history of heroic courage, of daring — coupled with research, reason, and relating. A record of another link in the Chain of Christianity — the outreach of the Gospel's path.

"I am proud to have done it for America. My reward will be your continued use of 'Air Mail'." — *Lindbergh*

Many years later, some thirteen, Lindbergh had an opportunity to look at his plane where it hung suspended in the Smithsonian Institution. Now a famous man, still serving his country, but suffering from the publicity which haunted him from the first, he stood behind the glass case containing a model of Martha Washington, featuring one of her historic gowns.

> No one took notice of me there, for if they looked at all it was at Martha Washington's dress, and not at me.... How strange it seemed, standing there looking at the plane, and what a chasm of time and circumstances separated us. Yet in another sense how close we still were! I could feel myself in the cockpit again, taking off from the rain-softened runway at Roosevelt Field, skimming low over the waves of mid-Atlantic, or brushing past a high peak of the Rockies. Such a little plane, it seemed to me today; I felt about it as I once felt about the Old Wright biplanes. Still, there was a trimness about the *Spirit of St. Louis* that even now gives me a feeling of pride. I felt I could take it down from its cables, carry it to some flying field, and feel perfectly at home in that cockpit again. (Charles A. Lindbergh, *The Wartime Journals of Charles A. Lindbergh,* Harcourt Brace Jovanovich, Inc., New York, 1970, pp. 319–320)

Charles Lindbergh is one of the quiet heroes of our century. His life of service to his nation, his own efforts in aviation and technology, his work in conservation, his life as a husband and father all testify to the quality of his character. Science and philosophy were his guiding lights first; then as the man deepened in his reflective study and work he became a man of Christian conviction. One biographer wrote about this aspect of the man:

When he went to Germany after the war, to survey German aviation and rocketry for the United States government, he brought with him his firsthand prewar knowledge that the Germans had been leaders in aeronautical science and manufacturing. He had admired them then for their efficiency, their energy, their scientific exactitude. Yet, with all this, he saw the evidence of their catastrophe, tragic and inescapable. It gave him a third new thought. It wasn't enough, Lindbergh reasoned, to be the first in science, or industry, or air power. "In Germany, I learned that if this civilization is to continue, modern man must direct the material power of his science by the spiritual truths of his God."

These three conclusions are remarkable because they come from Lindbergh. They are ideas he did not have before the war; they are not the *sort* of ideas he would have had before the war. And they are not just words; they are sincere, deeply felt changes in his attitude toward life.

He recognized this himself, "To me in youth," he wrote, "science was more important than either man or God. The one I took for granted; the other was too intangible for me to understand." Today, Lindbergh has lost his scientist's arrogance. And, as for God — God may be dead for some theologians, but not for Lindbergh. He has become a God-fearing man. (Ross, pp. 360–361)

Books by Charles A. Lindbergh: *The Spirit of St. Louis,* Macmillan, 1953 (Pulitzer Prize)**; *The Wartime Journals of Charles A. Lindbergh,* Harcourt Brace, 1970.

EDDIE RICKENBACKER: HERO OF WHEELS AND WINGS

by Fred M. Irvin

As we have said before, the twentieth century has been the century of *wheels* and *wings* — of transportation, especially in the development of the modern automobile and the modern plane. One man played a heroic role in both these fields.

Edward Rickenbacker, Eddie, was born in Columbus, Ohio in 1890, of parents who had emigrated to the United States from the German section of Switzerland. From his parents he learned hard work, purpose, and love of God and country. Eddie's school education was limited because when his father died he determined to help his mother by working fulltime for the meager wages available to a boy. But even a few dollars a week helped to feed and clothe the family of seven children. In his own words Eddie Rickenbacker described his first job at the Federal Glass Factory, working at night, and walking two miles to work:

> I walked all night long too, on the job. The factory made glass tumblers. Skilled glassblowers fashioned them from molten glass by lung power, one at a time. Then I carried them on a heavy, awkward steel platter with a long handle to the tempering ovens. When we stopped at midnight for lunch, my legs were tired, and I thought my arms were going to drop off. I had hardly finished my sandwich when it was time to go back to work again. Somehow I finished the night and walked the two miles home. I went to sleep eating breakfast.
>
> Payday eased the aches of tired muscles and made up for lost sleep. I had never thought to ask how much money I would receive. At the end of the first week, after six twelve-hour nights, I was given a small brown envelope. I

peeped inside. In it were three dollar bills and a silver half-dollar. I'd never seen so much money at one time in my life before, and I had earned every penny of it. I handed it to my mother and watched her eyes light up as she took out the small fortune.

It was the proudest day of my life.
(*Rickenbacker, An Autobiography*, Prentice-Hall, 1967, pp. 20–21)

Eddie was forced to give up school in the seventh grade for he could not keep up the grueling work and attend. He changed jobs many times trying to educate himself about engines. He became a mechanic and enrolled in a correspondence course in mechanical engineering which would include special instruction on gasoline engines.

Finally Eddie was able to help build some of the new automobiles being developed and to race them in competition to interest the American public in American cars. By 1915 Eddie had organized his own racing team and became known as a "speed king" earning prize money. It was a hazardous life. One night Eddie awoke from the dream of a crash. As he pondered all his brushes with death in his life he realized how fortunate he had been.

That night I re-evaluated my entire life. I seemed to me that surely the Lord above had shown a special interest in protecting me through so many hazardous experiences. It was about time, I realized, that I began to show some appreciation for this Divine consideration. The least I could do, in addition to keeping my faith steadfast, was to improve the condition of the body and mind that the Lord was obviously saving for some purpose.

I worked out a series of exercises, which I did — and do to this day — for fifteen minutes each morning and night to keep my body flexible.

I had always gone down my knees and prayed before going to bed each night, and I continued the practice with even greater sincerity and gratitude. I did not then, I am sorry to say, talk of my religion and attempt to inspire others. I doubt if any of the millions of spectators who saw me blasting around curves with controlled madness ever dreamed that I would be on my knees that night praying. (Rickenbacker, p. 65)

Eddie Rickenbacker was a man who endeavored to make every field he entered a better field of activity. For the field of racing he wrote a little booklet of rules and regulations — setting a high standard of character, work, and conduct so as not to reflect discredit on this means of earning a livelihood. Much of the information learned from automobile racing was translated into features of safety and excellence for passenger cars.

In 1916, Eddie Rickenbacker, whose name was now well known, was introduced to the second field he was to serve — the airplane. His first ride was with Glen Martin, founder of a famous company which built planes. Martin was just beginning his career and he gave Eddie his first plane ride. But it was not until World War I in France, through the efforts of Colonel William "Billy" Mitchell, America's great air pioneer, that he began to learn how to pilot a plane himself. Because of Eddie's remarkable persistence, practice, and determination, he was able to prepare himself as a combat pilot — in one year's time.

As one studies the life of Eddie Rickenbacker one learns what a fine leader of men he was. He had the ability to bind men together — and the willingness to do all the hard work of a "servant" rather than a master. His own skill with machines — first cars — now planes — earned him the title of the *American Ace of Aces*. In that daredevil era of individual air combat, Eddie Rickenbacker proved himself superior.

After the war Eddie Rickenbacker once again sought a time of quiet in order to determine how to use his life worthy of the Lord's protection.

> Alone under the stars, I readjusted my mind to serving mankind constructively in peace, rather than through destruction in war, and stabilized my nerves and physical condition. I had been living under great pressure for the past few years. In my continuing competition with the Grim Reaper, I had endured 134 aerial encounters in which other humans tried to shoot me down. I made no effort even to guess at the number of times I had been shot at. So many close calls renewed my thankfulness to the Power above, which had seen fit to preserve me. (Rickenbacker, p. 136)

Captain Eddie Rickenbacker was a hero now to both young and old. He knew that his personal conduct and character had to be irreproachable in order to keep their respect. He was asked to appear in a motion picture and a check was made out to him for $100,000. But although Eddie's resources were very low, he never considered the offer for he felt it would "degrade both my own stature and the uniform I so proudly wore." Eddie felt that the movies were not the best place to inspire or influence the youth of our country.

Eddie's earlier interest in automobiles convinced him that he should build an "automobile of my own design. In it I would incorporate all the new features and developments that automotive designers, engineers, and factories were then capable of producing. One of my reasons for changing racing cars so frequently had been to study the different designs and performances. In quiet days on the front I had thought about building an automobile — and building it under my name. In the quiet of the desert, I decided that what I wanted to do was to build the Rickenbacker automobile." (Rickenbacker, pp. 142-143)

The Rickenbacker Motor Company did well — and the car was designed for "anyone who recognized fine engineering and workmanship." Despite the early years of the depression, and with the intense sales efforts of Eddie himself, the car was a success. But four-wheel brakes proved to be his downfall. Because it was a new idea — for passenger cars — the other automobile companies attacked the idea as extremely dangerous. The Rickenbacker Company was not able to succeed over the adverse publicity. In two years Eddie was flat broke and owed $250,000.

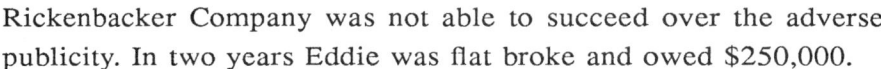
RICKENBACKER *Sport Phaeton*

> Several friends suggested that I declare bankruptcy, but I did not consider it for even a moment. I owed the money, and I would pay it back if I had to work like a dog to do it.
>
> I was not ashamed and not afraid. Failure was something I had faced before and might well face again. I have said it over and over: 'Failure' is the greatest word in the English language. Here in America failure is not the end of the world. If you have the determination, you can come back from failure and succeed. (Rickenbacker, p. 149)

At the same time as Eddie's company failed the President of a Detroit bank called him in and indicated that if he needed financing for a new line of endeavor to come and see him. Eddie knew once again that despite seeming failure God was still with him.

During the 1920s, Eddie, used to working eighteen-hour days, not only paid back his debt, but launched a number of other business enterprises — among them the Indianapolis Speedway. Through the operation of the Speedway the automotive and allied industries made great strides in their art.

But flying, too, was a continuing interest of Eddie Rickenbacker. Even in his automotive days of the Rickenbacker car he had designed a "simple, compact, star-shaped engine for a small plane." During the 1920's Eddie also kept alive his interests in all phases of aviation. The culmination of his interest in aviation was the purchase of Eastern Air Lines — an enterprise which required new dedication of his skills in building both an airline and in building the country's willingness to support the airlines with expanded airports.

One of Rickenbacker's goals was to operate Eastern without government subsidy — without taking taxpayer's money to keep it in business. It was the first airline to operate as a free enterprise company.

In 1941, Eddie Rickenbacker again had a battle with the Grim Reaper. On a trip from Birmingham the DC-3 in which he was traveling crashed. Even during the hours when he was pinned inside the wreckage with severe injuries he directed the passengers in rescue operations. During critical months in the hospital again and again he turned back Death — and found that only as he removed all drugs could he begin to feel the "natural recuperative powers" of the body reassert themselves.

Later, Eddie found out why God had put him through that terrible year of suffering. It was part of his appointed mission of service to others and to his country. In 1941 World War II began and Eddie was ready to once again serve his nation. When General "Hap" Arnold, commanding general of the U.S. Army Air Forces, called him for an important mission, he was ready.

> "I'll be there bright and early Monday morning," I said. Though I had no idea what job he had for me, I knew that it would be an important one, one related to the mission of the Air Forces in our fight for freedom. I thanked God for sparing me to fight again for America. War is hell, but sometimes a necessary hell. When it comes, everyone should be proud to give his services unflinchingly to his country. (Rickenbacker, p. 249)

Rickenbacker, who was one of the few men, along with Charles Lindbergh, who had seen and recognized Germany's growing military might, had tried in vain to arouse America to a state of preparedness. Rickenbacker believed World War II could have been prevented if America had converted to Air Power during 1935–1940. A strong America would have deterred both Germany and Japan.

During World War II Eddie Rickenbacker served America on a series of official and secret missions, both inside continental America and overseas. It was on a 1942 Pacific mission that Rickenbacker found out why God had preserved his life so many times in the past. During 23 days, with seven other men, he demonstrated the testimony of his ability to inspire other men with faith in God — and survive — on three life rafts in the ocean. This is one of the great stories of the twentieth century. It should be read in its entirety in

Rickenbacker's own words. For there were no atheists when seven of the eight came through — and every man's life was changed — even Rickenbacker's.

There were miracles during that unbelievable ordeal of almost four weeks — with no water — or food — or protection from the sun and the sea.

> It was clear to me that God had had a purpose in keeping me alive. It was to help the others, to bring them through. I had been saved to serve. It was an awesome responsibility, but I accepted it gladly and proudly. (Rickenbacker, p. 7)

Rickenbacker's account in his autobiography contains many heart-rending details of the long days and nights at sea. But the aspect of faith is most inspiring. Up to this time in his life Rickenbacker had kept his faith as a "quiet, personal thing.... Now, for the first time in all those years, I realized that I should share my faith with others and help them to find strength through God." Rickenbacker organized daily prayer and Bible study twice each day. Each man read from the Word, each man prayed, each man sang.

> We didn't know all the words, but we did the best we could. I encouraged the singing, and, when some of the men began to lose interest and faith, I'd sing louder, keeping time on the side of the raft, exhorting them all to join me. I never lost faith, not once, but it was sometimes necessary for me to rekindle faith in others.... There were some cynics and unbelievers among us. But not after the eighth day. For it was on that day that a small miracle occurred. (Rickenbacker, p. 316-317)

It was after prayer meeting, and the men were dozing in the oppressive heat. Rickenbacker was dressed in civilian clothes with a fedora hat, which protected his head from the sun. "Suddenly, something landed on my head. I knew that it was a sea gull, I don't know how I knew; I just knew." (Rickenbacker, p. 317)

And slowly, with all eyes watching him, Eddie caught the gull — and he became their first meal. Part of the gull was used for fish bait and two small fishes were caught. Later it rained and they caught rain in their clothes and wrung it into their mouths.

by Fred M. Irvin

But eight days had to extend into twenty-three — twenty-three terrible days of combating suffering, starvation, thirst, pain, illness, and the death of one man. There were also moments of temptation to end it all. Moments when planes flew overhead — and did not see them. Through it all Eddie Rickenbacker exercised all the skill God had taught him to keep the spirits and the faith of these men alive. Just as he had fought so many times to stay alive himself — he would not permit these men to give up, to wait for death.

> But I wouldn't permit that to happen. I continued the nightly prayer meetings and insisted that we continue trying to raise our cracked voices in song. I used every trick I knew on them. To some I spoke with encouragement; I was as soft and gentle as a mother. But others required stronger medicine. I rode them; I tore them to pieces; I struck at every raw nerve in their bodies. (Rickenbacker, p. 324)

In the end, when almost the whole world had written their obituary — they were sighted — a tiny dot in the South Pacific. There were painful days of recovery — but faith had won a great victory and immortal souls had been saved as well as rescued. Rickenbacker himself was a renewed man.

Some years later, writing to his son Bill he stated,

> There were all saved but one, and, surely they must have been saved for good reasons and the realization that their work was not yet completed.
>
> On the raft in the Pacific, we had two men on board who were atheists — Lt. Whittaker and Col. Adamson. Neither one of them believed in God; in fact, Whittaker had never been in a church or chapel or listened to a sermon until we arrived at the hospital in the Samoa Islands where they had a small chapel and I took him to his first service at his request because of what he saw transpire before his very eyes during those twenty-three hectic days and nights.
>
> Since his return to this country, he has given a great amount of his time to the service of God.
>
> And I shall never forget the letter — I have the original — from Colonel Adamson after I had brought him home and placed him in Walter Reed Hospital, in which he stated, 'Not only did you save a man, but you saved a lost soul.' (William F. Rickenbacker, *From Father to Son: the Letters of Captain Eddie Rickenbacker to His Son William, From Boyhood to Manhood,* Walker and Company: New York 1970, pp. 90-91)

Of all the changes brought about in those twenty-three days on the raft, the greatest change seemed to be in Eddie Rickenbacker himself. Up to this time in his life, as he stated, he had always been quiet about his faith. But after his deliverance which he ascribed to "the providence of the Lord above" he no longer had any hesitation about sharing his faith with others. Now it was an active and open part of his life. In effect Eddie Rickenbacker was a true evangelist with the testimony of his own life.

The Lord spared Eddie Rickenbacker for many more years of active service to Christ and country. This man of action, daring, and courage passed away quietly — with a blessed hope of heaven.

A Book for Younger Readers

Eddie Rickenbacker, Young Racer and Flyer, by Catherine Cleven, illustrated by Fred M. Irvin (1974), published by Bobbs-Merrill which produced the Childhood of Famous Americans series, (now with Macmillan), is no longer in print but may be found used or from libraries. It is an excellent book to read after you have properly introduced this man of faith and action to your family. Perhaps you can find some other biographies which are still available.

HEROINES IN OUR HISTORY

In the early history of our colonial period only a few names of heroic women are recorded — not because there were no heroic women — but rather that they played their role behind the scenes, quietly and effectively. Until women came as permanent settlers to Jamestown, Virginia, and until families were started, the men of Jamestown fared poorly. And the Princess Pocahontas, our first American Indian convert could not have received Christian instruction in the home of Alexander Whitaker had there not been women present in the colony with whom she could live.

Our Pilgrim history is filled with the evidence of womanly heroism. In his American Christian classic, *History 'Of Plimoth Plantation,'* William Bradford records the sufferings of the women as they became "strangers and pilgrims."

After several unsuccessful attempts to escape from England, a Dutchman had agreed to bring his ship close to shore between Grimsby and Hull. But a low tide prevented the women from getting on board. When the Dutch captain spied the sheriff's company coming to arrest the Pilgrims as religious dissenters, he lifted anchor and sailed away with a large complement of the Pilgrim men. They spent two weeks "enduring a fearfull storme at sea, being 14. days or more before they arrived at their port" in Holland. But God did Providentially deliver them, to the amazement of all.

Meanwhile the poor women and children, with a few men who stayed to help them, were carried about —

> "... from one place to another, and from one justice to another, till in the ende they knew not what to doe with them; for to imprison so many women & innocent children for no other cause (many of them) but that they must goe with their husbands, seemed to be unreasonable and all would crie out of them; and to send them home againe was as difficult, for they aledged, as the truth was, they had no homes to goe to, for they had either sould, or otherwise disposed of their houses & livings. To be shorte, after they had been thus turmolyed a good while, and conveyed from one constable to another, they were glad to be ridd of them in ye end upon any termes; for all were wearied & tired with them. Though in ye mean time they (poore soules) indured miserie enough; and thus in ye end necessitie forste a way for them." (*Christian History,* p. 188)

William Bradford records one of the most poignant passages in American Literature when the *Mayflower* dropped anchor off Cape Cod in November of 1620. The sixty-six day voyage across a stormy ocean had been difficult and now they looked upon another challenging physical barrier, an uninhabited wilderness.

> But hear I cannot but stay and make a pause, and stand half amased at this poore peoples presente condition; and so I thinke will the reader too, when he well considers ye same. Being thus passed ye vast ocean, and a sea of troubles before in their preparation (as may be remembered by yt which wente before), they had now no freinds to wellcome them, nor inns to entertaine or refresh their weather-

 beaten bodys, no houses or much less townes to repaire too, to seeke for succoure....

Besids, what could they see but a hidious & desolate wildernes, full of wild beasts & wild men? and what multituds ther might be of them they knew not.... For summer being done, all things stand upon them with a wetherbeaten face; and ye whole countrie, full of woods & thickets, represented a wild & savage heiw. If they looked behind them, ther was ye mighty ocean which they had passed, and was now as a maine barr & goulfe to separate them from all ye civill parts of ye world....

What could now sustaine them but ye spirite of God & his grace? May not & ought not the children of these fathers rightly say: Our faithers were Englishmen which came over this great ocean, and were ready to perish in this willdernes; but they cried unto ye Lord, and he heard their voyce, and looked on their adversitie &c. Let them therfore praise ye Lord, because he is good, & his mercies endure for ever....(*Christian History,* pp. 202–203)

PURITAN WIFE, MOTHER, POETESS: ANNE BRADSTREET

But what did the women of the early colonial period have to say for themselves about their own feelings as they faced the peculiar difficulties of a wilderness life? We know of the courage which the men demonstrated as they explored, as they set forth into the woods, not knowing if a savage foe lay in wait for them. We know how valiantly they worked when weak from the lack of food to build the meeting house and fort and the first dwellings needed for their families. But what about the demands made upon the Pilgrim and Puritan women?

Bradford's account of the Pilgrim women includes few names. But we do have the record of a remarkable Puritan woman whose own diary, journal, and writings give us an indication of the American Christian character which was being formed. Anne Dudley Bradstreet (1612–1672), daughter of one governor, Thomas Dudley, wife of another, Simon Bradstreet, has left us a legacy of her poetry and a unique testimony to the life of a Puritan woman in 17th century America. She was our first American poet.

Anne Bradstreet arrived with Governor John Winthrop and his fleet of six ships in 1630. She was with her father and husband of two years. Anne was eighteen years old. They came on the flagship *Arbella* with Lady Arbella and John Winthrop. Many years later she wrote of her feelings as she confronted life in the village of Salem where they first landed — four hundred new settlers, including children, servants, cattle, and many more supplies than the Pilgrims had enjoyed.

> I found a new world and new manners, at which my heart rose. But after I was convinced it was the way of God, I submitted to it and joined to the church at Boston.

Boston, named after the English city, became the site of the fast-growing Massachusetts Bay Colony — that colony which would finally include in 1690 the Old Colony of Plymouth.

Our Forefathers and Mothers from England brought us a unique heritage of education and government — the outcome of their Biblical knowledge. As Daniel Webster was to indicate many years later:

LIBERTY TREE, BOSTON
Patriots' Rallying Place

> Cultivated mind was to act on uncultivated nature; and more than all, a government and a country were to commence with the very first foundations laid under the divine light of Christianity.

Anne Bradstreet had enjoyed an education in the Bible, in history, in literature. She had studied in some of the great Puritan libraries of England, and family discussions in home, at table, and on board ship were of the subjects which had been occupying their minds. Thus her very first poems reflect the Pilgrim and Puritan knowledge of history and literature.

In *The Works of Anne Bradstreet*,* (republished in 1967 by The Belknap Press of Harvard University Press; edited by Jeannine Hensley, Foreword by Adrienne Rich), the following poems take up almost half the volume: *The Four Elements* (Fire, Air, Earth, and Water); *Of the Four Humours in Man's Constitution* (Choler, Blood, Melancholy, Phlegm) a medieval concept of personality; *The Four Ages of Man* (Childhood, Youth, Manly, and Old Age); *The Four Seasons of the Year* (Spring, Summer, Autumn, Winter); and *The Four Monarchies* (The Assyrian, The Persian, The Grecian, and The Roman). These poems done in the style of the times reflect Anne's education and her study of the French Calvinist poet, Du Bartas. They express the interest of our Puritan forebears in reflective learning — a quality which became the hallmark of New England.

But poems which a family can enjoy together are found in Anne Bradstreet's writings about her family and her life as a woman in early New England history. What did she think of her father, Thomas Dudley, from whom she had learned so much? Anne dedicates her book of poems to him in a first offering: "To Her Most Honoured Father, Thomas Dudley Esq. These Humbly Presented." Her 47-line poem ends with these last two lines:

> From her that to yourself more duty owes
> Then water in the boundless ocean flows.
> *March 20, 1642*   ANNE BRADSTREET

What does she think of her husband — father of her eight children? In one of the most beautiful of her verses she begins:

> *To My Dear and Loving Husband*
>
> If ever two were one, then surely we.
> If ever man were loved by wife, then thee.

> If ever wife was happy in a man,
> Compare with me, ye women, if you can....

Anne was a faithful mother, brooding and watching over her children as they experienced their own different states and stages. In one of her later poems she writes in part:

In Reference to Her Children, 23 June 1659

> I had eight birds hatched in one nest,
> Four cocks there were, and hens the rest.
> I nursed them up with pain and care,
> Nor cost, nor labour did I spare,
> Till at the last they felt their wing,
> Mounted the trees, and learned to sing...
>
> O would my young, ye saw my breast,
> And knew what thoughts there sadly rest,
> Great was my pain when I you bred,
> Great was my care when I you fed,
> Long did I keep you soft and warm,
> And with my wings kept off all harm,
> My cares are more and fears than ever,
> My throbs such now as 'fore were never....

Perhaps one of the greatest trials and tests of Anne's faith was in 1666 when her house burned down. It was difficult to reconcile the loss — not only of precious books and manuscripts, but of the furnishings brought so far by ocean voyage from England — comforts in this American wilderness. Yet the Puritan regarded all aspects of life as opportunities for growth in Christian maturity. And Anne Dudley Bradstreet, America's first poet, was ultimately able to lay her loss at the feet of her Heavenly Father. As she surveyed the ashes and ruins of her past life — recalling the places "where oft I sat and long did lie," as she remembered "here stood that trunk, and there that chest, There lay that store I counted best" — she knew that the pleasant life of the past was no more. No guests should eat under her roof, nor should the "bridegroom's voice e'er heard shall be."

GOVERNOR SIMON BRADSTREET HOUSE
WHERE ANNE BRADSTREET LIVED

But "that mighty Architect" had another house framed for her, "with glory richly furnished" and "permanent though this be fled." And best of all: "It's purchased and paid for too by Him who hath enough to do." So Anne looked up, not down, for her future "treasure" and stated as a good Puritan believer:

> The world no longer let me love,
> My hope and treasure lies above.

Anne Dudley Bradstreet was a heroine — an American Christian heroine — an English Puritan transplanted to New England, willing to shape and form a new life, and able to let her talents of mind or heart blossom on the vine. As her biographer, Adrienne Rich, states in the Foreword of the Harvard edition of her poems:

Anne Bradstreet happened to be one of the first American women, inhabiting a time and a place in which heroism was a necessity of life.... To find room in that life for any mental activity, which did not directly serve certain spiritual ends, was an act of great self-assertion and vitality. To have written poems, the first good poems in America, while rearing eight children, frequently lying sick, and keeping house at the edge of the wilderness, was to have managed a poet's range and extension within confines as severe as any American poet has confronted.

Perhaps Anne Bradstreet best put the position which God allowed for American women into her own words. She resisted the designation that women could only fulfill domestic functions and could not also, without neglecting woman's most critical role of forming the character of the next generation, exercise intellectual talents. At the same time she fully accepted the role of masculine headship of home and church, and meekly acknowledged "what every woman knows" — that women's accomplishments only enhance the character of men.

From *The Prologue*

5

I am obnoxious to each carping tongue
Who says my hand a needle better fits,
A poet's pen all scorn I should thus wrong,
For such despite they cast on female wits:
If what I do prove well, it won't advance,
They'll say it's stol'n, or else it was by chance.

7

Let Greeks be Greeks, and women what they are
Men have precedency and still excel,
It is but vain unjustly to wage war;
Men can do best, and women know it well.
Preeminence in all and each is yours;
Yet grant some small acknowledgement of ours.

8

And oh ye high flown quills that soar the skies,
And ever with your prey still catch your praise,
If e'er you deign these lowly lines your eyes,
Give thyme or parsley wreath, I ask no bays;
This mean and unrefined ore of mine
Will make your glist'ring gold but more to shine.

Anne Bradstreet's poems were published in England in 1750 by her brother-in-law who had secretly carried her manuscript with him, without her knowledge. The title was selected by him, *The Tenth Muse, Lately Sprung Up in America*. Today we honor Anne Bradstreet as our first American poet. It is a testimony to the Westward course of the Gospel as it opened up new opportunities for Christian character, education, and government — the liberty and productivity of the individual.

HEROINES OF THE AMERICAN REVOLUTION: LYDIA DARRAH AND OTHERS

While the physical strength of women does not equal that of most men, they are often equal in courage. There are a number of accounts of women's courage during the American Revolution that thrill our hearts to read. It can remind us of what is required of character and commitment to perpetuate our American Christian Republic.

The year seventeen hundred and seventy-seven was a critical year for the American forces — those "ragged Continentals." This was the winter when George Washington and his troops witnessed God bring life out of death at Valley Forge. Just forty miles away the British occupied the city of Philadelphia and enjoyed warmth, food, and shelter, while Americans starved and shivered with cold in their inadequate huts. Yet even in the city there were hearts determined not to give the enemy any advantage. Lydia Darrah was one woman whose heart was faithful to Christ and country.

William and Lydia Darrah were Quakers and members of the Society of Friends. They were devoted to the principles of non-violence. The house of Lydia and her husband was often used for private conferences by the British officers for it was immediately opposite the headquarters of General Howe who was in charge of the occupation. Lydia had been cautioned by a British officer that a meeting was to be held in her home and that the family should all be in bed at an early hour. Lydia followed his precautions and retired herself, without undressing.

GENERAL HOWE'S HEADQUARTERS

Elizabeth F. Ellet, writing in her book *The Women of the American Revolution,* described Lydia's quandry:

> But sleep refused to visit her eyelids. Her vague apprehensions gradually assumed more definite shape. She became more and more uneasy, till her nervous restlessness amounted to absolute terror. Unable longer to resist the impulse — not of curiosity, but surely of a far higher feeling — she slid from the bed, and taking off her shoes, passed noiselessly from her chamber and along the entry. Approaching cautiously the apartment in which the officers were assembled she applied her ear to the key-hole. For a few moments she could distinguish but a word or two amid the murmur of voices; yet what she did hear but stimulated her eager desire to learn the important secret of the conclave.
>
> At length there was profound silence, and a voice was heard reading a paper aloud. It was an order for the troops to quit the city on the night of the fourth, and march out to a secret attack upon the American army, then encamped at White Marsh.
>
> Lydia had heard enough and she returned to her room and bed. Later she let out the officers and "fastened the house, and extinguished the lights and fire." Now came the time of testing. There was no sleep or repose for her that night. How could she help her country and not jeopardize the safety of her husband and family? How could she warn the American army of the danger that threatened their lives? Lydia prayed for God's guidance and direction. She knew at last that she must "encounter this risk alone."

Lydia's plan was to warn the army at White Marsh, but she proceeded to carry out her intention by an ordinary strategem. At daybreak she informed her husband that she was going to walk to Frankford to obtain flour which she needed for the household. In order to pass the British Lines she secured written permission from General Howe. Lydia had no difficulty reaching the flour mill — but it was at this point that she was commencing the dangerous part of her mission. After leaving her bag at the mill she "pressed forward with all haste towards the outposts of the American Army. Her determination was to apprise General Washington of the danger."

Lydia met just the right American officer — on official recognizance to learn the enemy's plans. This officer recognized Lydia Darrah. "To him she disclosed the secret, after having obtained from him a solemn promise not to betray her individually, since the British might take vengeance on her and her family."

The culmination of this courageous mission was when Lydia had to appear before the British officer who had arranged the meeting in her home. She was able to reply truthfully that her family were all asleep.

> "It is very strange"...said the officer, and mused a few minutes. "You, I know, Lydia, were asleep; for I knocked at your door three times before you heard me — yet it is certain that we were betrayed. I am altogether at a loss to conceive who could have given the information of our intended attack to General Washington! On arriving near his encampment we found his cannon mounted, his troops under arms, and so prepared at every point to receive us, that we have been compelled to march back without injuring our enemy, like a parcel of fools."

BRITISH SURRENDER AT YORKTOWN

Lydia Darrah rejoiced and blessed the Lord that she had not had to utter an untruth in her defense — and that her warning had preserved and prevented the destruction of many men and lives — not only of her own nation, but the lives of the enemy, too. This inspiring example of Lydia Darrah and that of several other women from different sections of the country can be found in the section "Patriotic Women and Home Sentiment" in *The Christian History of the American Revolution: Consider and Ponder* by Verna M. Hall, published by F.A.C.E.

The American Christian Homes in Our Republic were homes where the character to support a nation was shaped and formed by parents whose love of Christ and country helped us win the war for Independence. Here the unique talents of a Christian woman played a critical role in the history of the nation. As Mrs. Ellet writes (*C&P*, p. 73):

> Patriotic mothers nursed the infancy of freedom. Their counsels and their prayers mingled with the deliberations that resulted in a nation's assertion of its independence. They animated the courage, and confirmed the self-devotion of those who ventured all in the common cause.... They willingly shared inevitable dangers and privations.... It is almost impossible now to appreciate the vast influence of woman's patriotism upon the destinies of the infant republic.

DOMESTIC HEROINE: MERCY OTIS WARREN

Courage was required by women from the time of our earliest Colonial settlements — special courage, not only against the difficult physical circumstances of life but for the particular demands upon women as wives and mothers, as educators of the next generation. And America was indeed the culmination of "the most complete expression of the Christian civilization." Here women could fulfill the standard set for them in the first century of Christianity when Paul carried the Gospel on its westward course — from Asia, "the continent of beginnings" — to Europe, "the continent of development."

One of the most important steps for America's Christian History occurred in Acts 16 when the Apostle Paul, heeding the Macedonian Cry, turned westward to the Continent of Europe. At Philippi, "which is the chief city of that part of Macedonia, and a colony" Paul found his first European convert in Lydia "a seller of purple, of the city of Thyatira." Lydia's words after her baptism have significance for the new life now opened up for women — a life whose unique role and contribution comes to particular fruition in the United States of America.

> And when she was baptized, and her household, she besought us, saying, If ye have judged me to be faithful to the Lord, come into my house, and abide there. And she constrained us. (Acts 16:15)

Reverends W. J. Conybeare and J. S. Howson, in their *The Life and Epistles of Saint Paul,* American Edition of 1869, say this:

> Thus the Gospel had obtained a home in Europe... and nothing could be more calm and tranquil than its first beginnings on the shore of that continent, which it has long overspread. The scenes by the river-side, and in the house of Lydia, are beautiful prophecies of the holy influence which women, elevated by Christianity to their true position, and enabled by Divine grace to wear "the ornament of a meek and quiet spirit," have now for centuries exerted over domestic happiness and the growth of piety and peace.

America's Christian History begins the first history of any nation where the role of Christian women was so important. Defined by Lydia Sigourney in an article entitled "To Young Women" which can be found on pp. 407–410 in *The Christian History of the Constitution of the United States of America,* compiled by Verna M. Hall, we read:

> The natural vocation of females is to teach.... It is in the domestic sphere, in her own native province, that woman is inevitably a teacher. There she modifies by her example, her dependants, her companions, every dweller under her own roof. Is not the infant in its cradle her pupil?

Mrs. Sigourney, an excellent example of an American Christian woman in 19th century literature, then goes on to detail this important role of women, with particular emphasis upon the consequences of her influence in the nation:

> This influence is most visible and operative in a republic.... Teachers under such a form of government should be held in the highest honour. They

be the allies of legislators. They have agency in the prevention of crime. They aid in regulating the atmosphere, whose incessant action and pressure causes the life blood to circulate, and return pure and healthful to the heart of the nation.

On page 355 of *The Christian History of the American Revolution: Consider and Ponder,* compiled by Verna M. Hall, appears the portrait of Mercy Warren by John Singleton Copley, outstanding American Christian artist of the eighteenth century. The portrait reveals a woman of charm, intellect and of firm Christian character. While Mercy Otis Warren was the most notable American Woman of Letters during the Revolutionary and Constitutional period of our country — her first sphere of influence was as a faithful wife and mother, a teacher in the home.

Born in Barnstable, Massachusetts, on September 25, 1728, some one hundred years after the Pilgrims' arrival, Mercy Otis received no special schooling. Like the Pilgrims it was education in the home. Had it not been for her own enterprise and determination her routine of domestic activities would not have included the study and reading which characterize her early years. Never neglecting the cultivation of domestic skills which all Colonial girls were expected to master, nor the duties of hospitality, she still found time to improve her mind as well as to use her hands in various works of female ingenuity.

Mercy was supplied with books from the library of the local minister, Reverend Jonathan Russell. He counseled and guided her first study. Through her brother, James Otis, she became interested in the subject of history and discovered its relationship to character. Later, when writing her three volume *History of the rise, Progress and Termination of the American Revolution,* she made character a key to the study of history. James Otis became a patriot of renown during the difficult years in Massachusetts when England began to turn away from her own constitutional history. His *Rights of the British Colonies Asserted and Proved,* written in 1764 began the ten-year Constitutional debate prior to the American Revolution.

In 1754 Mercy Otis married James Warren, young merchant of Plymouth, and descendant of Richard Warren who came over on the *Mayflower.* James Warren became active in political events early in his career and served long and faithfully as President of the Massachusetts Provincial Assembly and as Paymaster General of the Continental Army.

Because discussion of principles and ideas was part of home life and was an important aspect of home education for all members of the family, Mercy became a friend and a correspondent of many leading political figures of her day. She exchanged ideas with John Adams, Samuel Adams, Thomas Jefferson, and Elbridge Gerry. She wrote poetry, but she also wrote a famous play, a political satire of the events in Massachusetts which were precipitating the American Revolution. Character was the key to *The Group,* written in 1775.

But even while Mercy Warren was writing innumerable letters, she was also running the farm in her husband's absence and bringing up their five sons, educating them in principles of Biblical and historical liberty so that they might become able defenders of the country which God was bringing into existence.

Here are some examples of the letters which Mercy Warren wrote to her husband while he was absent from home and his response to her. They indicate their deep and mutual love for each other, for their children, and for their God and country. It is in the correspondence of the American Revolutionary period that we see the importance of woman's role in our republic. It is in this correspondence that we see that quality of the American Christian woman whose strength and influence was first indicated in the words of Lydia to the Apostle Paul: "Come into my house, and abide there." (Acts 16:15)

LETTERS FROM MERCY TO JAMES

Plymouth, September 21, 1775

...Just as I (got) up from dinner this day yours of the 15 & 18 came to hand; No desert was ever more welcome to a luxurious pallate, it was a regale to my longing mind: I had been eagerly looking for more than a week for a line from the best friend of my heart.

I had contemplated to spend a day or two with my good father, but as you talk of returning so soon I shall give up that and every other pleasure this world can give for the superior pleasure of your company. I thank you for the many expressions in yours which bespeak the most affectionate soul, or heart warmed with friendship & esteem which it shall ever be my assiduous care to merit. — but as I am under some apprehensions that you will be again disappointed and your return postponed, I will endeavor to give you some account of the reception I met from our little family on my arrival among them after an absence which they thought long: your requesting this as an agreeable amusement is new proof that the Father is not lost in the occupations of the statesman.

I found Charles & Henry sitting on the steps of the front door when I arrived — they had just been expressing their ardent wishes to each other that mamah would come in before dinner when I turned the corner having our habitation.... George's solemn brow was covered with pleasure & his grave features not only danced in smiles but broke into a real laugh more expressive of his heartfelt happiness than all the powers of language could convey and before I could sit down and lay aside my riding attire all the choice gleanings of the Garden were offered each one pressing before the other to pour the yellow produce into their mamah's lap.

Not a complaint was uttered — not a tale was told through the day but what they thought would contribute to the happiness of their best friend; but how short lived is human happiness. The ensuing each one had his little grievance to repeat, as important to them as the laying an unconstitutional tax to the patriot or the piratical seizure of a ship & cargo, after much labour & the promising expectation of profitable returns when the voyage was compleat — but the umpire in your absence soon accommodated all matters to mutual satisfaction and the day was spent in much cheerfulness encircled by my sons.
...My heart has just leaped in my bosom and I ran to the stairs imagining I heard both your voice & your footsteps in the entry. Though disappointed I have no doubt this pleasure will be realized as soon as possible by

Your affectionate
M. WARREN

September 13, 1776

...my dearest friend, the best friend of my heart...

...When my head was layed on my pillow Last Night my Heart was Rent with Apprehension. Your life is of Great Value Both to the public & to the family as well as to the one who would be Miserable without you....I desire therefore to leave you in the Care of Providence & to trust in the divine protection to guard and guide your steps whithersoever you go.

I fear this people have been too confident of their own strength. We have been Ready to say our own arms shall save us instead of looking to the God of Battle....I shall write again tomorrow knowing you will not be tired of seeing the signature of your Beloved &

              Affectionate
              MARCIA

Dont think I am discouraged...when I write my thought so freely and fully. I seem to feel this day & Evening amidst a thousand gloomy fears as if our God was about to bring us deliverance by means which we cannot foresee. The less we have to hope from man the stronger is my confidence in Him who presideth over the Earth and who will be Glorifyed in His doing, and many times when we are Ready to say with Peter Lord help for we are sinking then is His arm stretched out to save....

LETTERS FROM JAMES TO MERCY
(His "saint, little angel, his beloved, he misses her beyond expectation.")

April 7, 1775 (a few days before Lexington)

The moving of the Inhabitants of Boston if Effected will be one Grand Move....we may perhaps be forced to Move: if we are let us strive to submit to the dispensations of Providence with Christian resignation & Phylosophick dignity. God has given you great abilities. You have improved them in great Acquirements. You are possessd of Eminent Virtues & distinguished Piety. For all these I Esteem I Love you in a degree that I can't Express. They are all now to be called into action for the good of mankind for the good of your friends, for the promotion of virtue and patriotism. Don't let the fluttering of your Heart Interrupt your Health or disturb your repose. Believe me I am continually Anxious about you. Ride when the weather is good & don't work or read too much at other times. I must bid you adieu. God Almighty Bless You no letter yet what can it mean, is she not well she can't forget me or have any objections to writing....

1779

If you Love me Enjoy the Goods of Providence with a Chearful Grateful Mind and at least imagine that our Lines are in a pleasant place.

Boston, April 2, 1780

My dear Mercy, — I am just returned from public worship, the next act of religion is to write to my beloved wife....Don't however think I am in the shades of gloom & despondency. I see & find difficulties from every quarter but my faith & Hope are as strong as ever....

READING ABOUT MERCY WARREN

In the 1890s an excellent series of six biographies was printed by Charles Scribner's Sons, New York. Entitled *Women of Colonial and Revolutionary Times,* it included biographies of Margaret Winthrop, Mercy Warren, Martha Washington, Catherine Schuyler, Dolly Madison, and Eliza Pinckney. These books, of course, are not still in print, but sometimes they can still be found in libraries, or in old bookstores for your purpose. The biography of Mercy Warren is entitled *Mercy Warren* by Alice Brown, Charles Scribner's Sons, New York, 1893.

In *The Christian History of the American Revolution: Consider and Ponder,* compiled by Verna M. Hall, there is a brief biography of Mercy Warren on pp. 76–77. Also in the same volume can be found 65 pages from Mrs. Warren's *History of the Rise, Progress and Termination of the American Revolution* which was first published in 1805. This excerpt from her writings begins on page 353 where she is identified as "Mercy Otis Warren, New England Historian Cotemporary with the American Revolution." On page 355 is Mercy's portrait by John Singleton Copley and pp. 357–422 contain her history. Mrs. Warren's account of the American Revolution is followed by a similar account by "David Ramsey, Southern Historian Cotemporary with the American Revolution." His portrait by Rembrandt Peale provides us with another example of the high quality of American Art during this period.

With these two accounts of history covering the same period we can see both a unity of emphasis and a diversity of style. All sections of the American colonies were nurtured and educated in the Bible. They accepted the Providential Approach to history. No wonder then that their accounts of events reflect their education and conviction of God's sovereignty in the affairs of men and nations.

In Mercy Warren's account of the American Revolution we are struck by her attention to character as the key to history and her understanding of the principles of government and the contrast between Christian self-government and arbitrary government.

From her *Introductory Observations,* we quote the following from Mercy Warren (see *Consider and Ponder,* pp. 358–360):

> The study of the human character opens at once a beautiful and deformed picture of the soul.... Thus when we look over the theatre of human action, scrutinize the windings of the heart, and survey the transactions of man from the earliest to the present period, it must be acknowledged that ambition and avarice are the leading springs which generally actuate the restless mind. From these primary sources of corruption have arisen all the rapine, and confusion, the depredation and ruin, that have spread distress over the face of the earth from the days of Nimrod to Cesar, and from Cesar to an arbitrary prince of the house of Brunswick....
>
> The love of domination and an uncontrolled lust of arbitrary power have prevailed among all nations, and perhaps in proportion to the degrees of civilization. They have been equally conspicuous in the decline of Roman virtue, and in the dark pages of British history.... It was the prevalence of them that drove the first settlers of America from elegant habitations and affluent circum-

THE CHAIN OF CHRISTIANITY MOVING WESTWARD WITH LIBERTY AND LAW

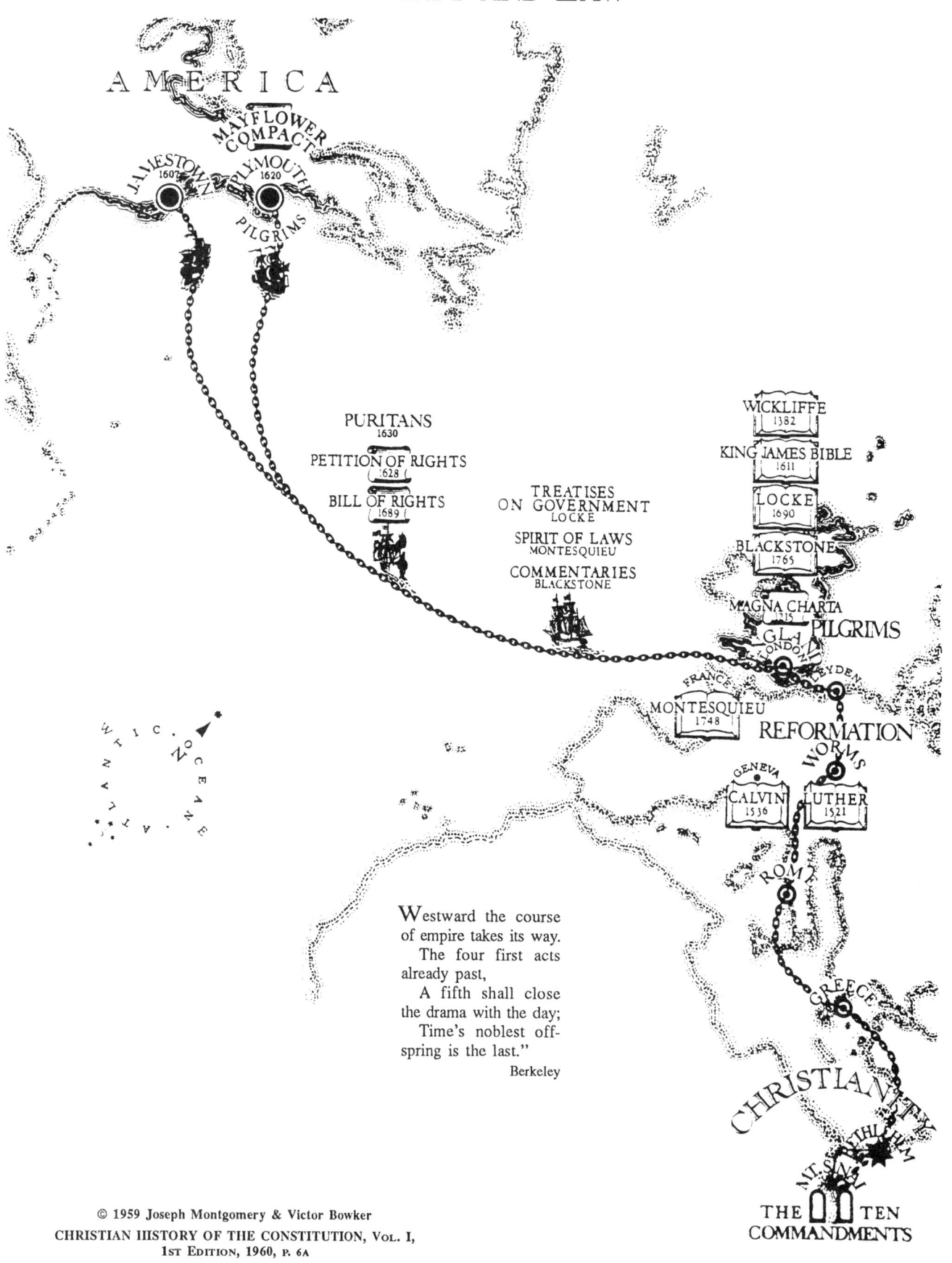

© 1959 Joseph Montgomery & Victor Bowker
CHRISTIAN HISTORY OF THE CONSTITUTION, VOL. I,
1ST EDITION, 1960, P. 6A

stances, to seek an asylum in the cold and uncultivated regions of the western world. Oppressed in Britain by despotic kings, and persecuted by prelatic fury, they fled to a distant country, where the desires of men were bounded by the wants of nature; where civilization had not created those artificial cravings which too frequently break over every moral and religious tie for their gratification.

It may seem remarkable to us that a woman would undertake to write one of our first histories of the American Revolution. Was Mercy Warren a *feminist,* a word derived from *feminism,* not found in Noah Webster's early 1828 *Dictionary?*

Feminism includes in its definition: 2. "The theory, cult, or practice of those who advocate such legal and social changes as will establish political, economic, and social equality of the sexes."

One has only to read the letters exchanged between Mercy Warren and her husband James, between John and Abigail Adams, to determine what devoted wives and mothers these two women were. They believed that their husbands would continue to identify in American government the opportunities for all individuals, men and women of all backgrounds and races, to be productive and to glorify the Lord with the proper development of the individual talents. As Abigail Adams reminded John Adams, when the *Declaration of Independence* was being written, "Remember the Ladies, and be more generous and favourable to them than your ancestors. Do not put such unlimited power into the hands of the Husbands. Remember all Men would be tyrants if they could.... Why then, not put it out of the power of the vicious and the Lawless to use us with cruelty and indignity with impunity. Men of Sense in all Ages abhor those customs which treat us only as the vassals of your Sex. Regard us then as Beings placed by providence under your protection and in immitation of the Supreem Being make use of that power only for our happiness."

ABIGAIL ADAMS

JOHN ADAMS

(Butterfield, L.H., Editor, *The Book of Abigail and John, Selected Letters of the Adams Family, 1762–1784,* Harvard University Press, 1975, p. 121)

It is quite evident that John Adams and James Warren regarded Abigail and Mercy as "beings placed by providence" under their protection. They also considered them highly qualified to discuss the events of their times in the light of the Biblical and political principles which were being debated. They were both confident of the devotion and capability of their wives as well as highly pleased with their interest and their participation, both through conversation and correspondence, in the great developments of the American Revolution.

As Mercy Warren began her *History* she clearly identified her own recognition of the distinctives of male and female:

> At a period when every manly arm was occupied, and every trait of talent or activity engaged, either in the cabinet or the field...I have been induced to improve the leisure Providence had lent, to record as they passed, in the following pages, the new and unexperienced events exhibited in a land previously blessed with peace, liberty, simplicity, and virtue.

Mercy Warren then went on to indicate her unusual sources through her family and husband which had connected her to "the most influential characters on the continent" which had given her access to "the best means of information" for her book. But she is ready to acknowledge that though she may seem to be venturing into a field hitherto identified as a masculine field, yet she cannot separate the domestic scene from the importance of "civil and religious liberty." Particularly in America the role of mothers as teachers and as formers and shapers of "the character of the next generation" is critical. Convinced that "all political attentions" did not "lay out of the road of female life" she continues:

> It is true there are certain appropriate duties assigned to each sex; and doubtless it is the more peculiar province of masculine strength, not only to repel the bold invader of the rights of his country and mankind, but in the nervous style of manly eloquence, to describe the blood-stained field, and relate the story of slaughtered armies.
>
> Sensible of this, the trembling heart has recoiled at the magnitude of the undertaking, and the hand often shrunk back from the task; yet, recollecting that every domestic enjoyment depends on the unimpaired possession of civil and religious liberty, that a concern for the welfare of society ought equally to glow in every human breast, the work was not relinquished....

JOSEPH WARREN AT BUNKER HILL

> With an expanded heart, beating with high hopes of the continued freedom and prosperity of America, the writer indulges a modest expectation, that the following pages will be perused with kindness and candor; this she claims, both in consideration of her sex, the uprightness of her intentions, and the fervency of her wishes for the happiness of all the human race.
>
> MERCY WARREN
Plymouth, Mass.
March, 1805

Let us pray that we in the twentieth and twenty-first centuries may once again raise up a generation that will include domestic heroines of the character and capability of Mercy Otis Warren!

PRESERVERS OF OUR HISTORY: ANN PAMELA CUNNINGHAM AND THE MOUNT VERNON LADIES' ASSOCIATION OF THE UNION

In 1853, the night boat had gone down the Potomac from Alexandria, carrying its usual crowd of travelers. About ten miles below the city, the ship's bell began to toll dolefully. The boat went slowly past Mount Vernon mansion. Ghostly, gaunt, and gray it stood, an ominous sight, enfolded in river mist, and lighted by the moon.

Among the passengers was Mrs. Robert Cunningham, of South Carolina, who had visited Mount Vernon when she was a child. Then it had been a stately white mansion, its lawn cut, and its shrubbery trimmed. She saw that unless something were done quickly, the famous old house would fall into ruins, its grounds be overrun by brambles and briars. Yet who should take the responsibility of its care, she wondered. Suddenly she thought, it is the *women* of America who should repair and preserve Mount Vernon — mansion, grounds, and tomb.[1]

Mrs. Robert Cunningham wrote to her invalid daughter describing her feelings as she gazed on the moonlit scene, and "she expressed her own thoughts about the preservation of Mount Vernon."

"I was painfully distressed at the ruin and desolation of the home of Washington, and the thought passed through my mind: Why was it that the women of this country did not try to keep it in repair, if the men could not do it? It does seem such a blot on our country!"[2]

RUINS AT MOUNT VERNON FROM 1835 FIRE
Sketch by Benson Lossing

As Miss Pamela Cunningham finished reading her mother's letter, she exclaimed, "I will do it!" All of the strength and enthusiasm she had put into physical living, before a fall from her horse had made her an invalid, she put into planning a way to buy and maintain Mount Vernon. She wrote letters addressed to the *Women of America* and sent them to a newspaper. To these she signed herself *The Southern Matron*. Through her untiring efforts she founded the Mount Vernon Ladies Association, and became its first Regent. Brilliant, talented, sincere women stepped forward from each state to assist her, and became the first Vice-Regents. The owner, John Augustine Washington, agreed to sell the mansion and 202 surrounding acres for $200,000.[3]

Miss Pamela Cunningham was a heroine who truly complemented American Christian manhood. For from her couch of invalidism she began "to emerge from her sheltered life and participate openly in public affairs." Certainly she could not be accused of "personal ambition" in her efforts to make the cause of our national shrine a national concern — especially among the women of the Union. In the truest sense of American Chris-

---

[1] Muir, Dorothy Troth, *Presence of a Lady, Mount Vernon 1861–1868,* Mount Vernon Ladies' Association, Mount Vernon, Virginia 1975, p. 1.
[2] Thane, Elswyth, *Mount Vernon is Ours, The Story of Its Preservation,* New York, Duell, Sloan and Pearce, 1966, p. 16.
[3] Muir, *Presence of a Lady,* pp. 7–8.

tian womanhood she first brought forth her counterpart from every state of the nation. The Mount Vernon Ladies Association is the oldest organization of its kind. It antedates the Daughters of the American Revolution (the D.A.R.) and the Colonial Dames, by more than thirty years. The Williamsburg Restoration is its junior by some seventy years. The Mount Vernon Ladies' Association is sixty-three years older than the National Park Service.

ANN PAMELA CUNNINGHAM

The Mount Vernon Ladies' Association is not sponsored by nor beholden to the Federal Government or the State of Virginia. It stands alone, its original charter having been granted in 1858, when ladies were not supposed to be capable of conducting anything like public affairs, and it was the creation of one resolute woman who at the age of thirty-seven acquired what even her friends at first considered an impracticable obsession. She had made up her mind that the home which George Washington loved should not be allowed to fall down in ruins from neglect. Not the uncooperative Washington family, the skeptical Virginia Legislature, nor her own condition of chronic invalidism could daunt her, nor swerve her from her apparently impossible purpose. As an example of sheer grit and courage, laced with Southern charm, Ann Pamela Cunningham remains unique.[4]

American philanthropy is known the world over and today the sum of $200,000 seems small in comparison with the great amounts of money contributed to the many causes which appeal for support. In the 1850s money was more difficult to come by and Americans had little experience with public appeals for funds. But help was at hand. Miss Cunningham knew "there there would have to be masculine know-how" in the areas of publicity, finance, and legalities. Writes Elswyth Thane, "Again she chose and got the best."

The best was "the Reverend and Honorable Dr. Edward Everett, Ph.D., Phi Beta Kappa, Member of Congress, Governor of Massachusetts, Minister to Great Britain, United States Senator, President of Harvard, pastor of various churches, and greatest of the Silver Tongues of his generation."[5]

And Edward Everett was enlisted in the cause of saving Mount Vernon. Willingly he became "the rod and staff without which even Miss Cunningham must have failed."

Divine Coincidences in the Mount Vernon Story

In 1855 Edward Everett considered that his major work was done and considered that with his own wife's invalidism he would be in semi-retirement. He still was in demand as a speaker and in 1855 accepted an invitation by the Mercantile Library Association of Boston to speak on February 22, 1856, on the *Character of Washington*. This speech or

---

[4] Thane, *Mount Vernon is Ours,* p. 3.
[5] Johnson, Gerald W. and Charles Cecil Wall, *Mount Vernon, The Story of a Shrine,* Mount Vernon Ladies' Association, Mount Vernon, Virginia, 1953, p. 12.

oration, as it was called in those days, became the open door to a new career. As Elswyth Thane writes:

> His Washington oration lasted nearly two hours, and was a great success. Possibly a sample of this popular form of rhetoric is pertinent here. More people knew Everett by this one oration than by any other, and it provided him with a springboard to appeal for national unity in troubled times, a subject very close to his heart. He was not by any means a spur-of-the-moment speaker — he left nothing to inspiration. It was all written out beforehand, as though for the printer. After careful study, he relied on his memory for delivery. He always carried his manuscript on to the platform with him, and then never referred to it. People complained sometimes that he was too perfect. It went like this:
>
>
> EDWARD EVERETT
>
> "A great and venerated character like that of Washington, which commands the respect of an entire population, however divided on other questions, is not an isolated fact in history to be regarded with barren admiration — it is a dispensation of Providence for good. It was well said by Mr. Jefferson in 1792, writing to Washington to dissuade him from declining a second nomination: 'North and South will hang together while they have you to hang to.'
>
> "Washington in the flesh is taken from us; we shall never behold him as our fathers did; but his memory remains, and I say let us hang to his memory. Let us make a national festival and holiday of his birthday; and ever, as the 22nd of February returns, let us remember, that while with these solemn and joyous rites of observance we celebrate the great anniversary, our fellow-citizens on the Hudson, on the Potomac, from the Southern plains to the Western lakes are engaged in the same offices of gratitude and love. Nor we, nor they alone — beyond the Ohio, beyond the Mississippi, along that stupendous train of immigration from East to West, which, bursting into States as it moves westward, is already threading the Western prairies, swarming through the portals of the Rocky Mountains and winding down their slopes, the name and the memory of Washington on that gracious night will travel with the silver queen of heaven through sixty degrees of longitude, nor part company with her till she walks in her brightness through the Golden Gate of California, and passes serenely on to hold midnight court with her Australian stars. There, and there only, in barbarous archipelagos, as yet untrodden by civilized man, the name of Washington is unknown, and there, too, when they swarm with enlightened millions, new honors will be paid to his memory."[6]

The word of Edward Everett's Oration on George Washington spread and a number of cities wanted to hear it. Meanwhile Everett himself suggested that he repeat his Washington Oration for the benefit of the Mount Vernon Fund. It was at this time that Rev. Everett first met Miss Cunningham, March 10, 1856. It was also at this time that she and the

---

[6] Thane, *Mount Vernon is Ours,* pp. 33-35.

Mount Vernon Ladies were working to have their organization chartered by the Virginia Legislature. She recorded her meeting with Edward Everett in the following words:

> Mr. Everett called to see me en route to Richmond and the spirit moved me on that day! I wondered at myself, when the excitement was over; but the end was gained! He consecrated that address from that moment to Mount Vernon. All was now prosperous....

A number of events were now coming together to make the efforts in the Mount Vernon crusade effective. With the publicity of Everett's Oration on George Washington national attention was focused. Also, just one year before in 1855, the first two volumes of Washington Irving's biography *Life of Washington* had appeared and was widely received and read — with anticipation of the volumes still to come. Irving himself was an enthusiastic supporter of the Mount Vernon restoration.

Edward Everett arrived in Richmond to give his first oration just at the moment when the battle for the Mount Vernon Ladies Association's charter was coming up for consideration in the Virginia Legislature. Judge Berrien, of Georgia, had suggested the creation of a non-profit corporation under the laws of Virginia.

The document for the charter had been drawn up and an influential member of the Virginia House, Mr. Langfitt, had promised to present the bill at the first opportunity. But after many weeks with the session moving to its close, no action had been taken. Anna Cora Ritchie, who was literally the campaign manager of the Mount Vernon campaign, took matters into her own competent hands. With the help of her husband, she invited many members of the Legislature, and many Senators of Virginia to her own home in Richmond. The subject was brought up to the Governor, and he pledged to personally use his best endeavors to pass the bill — *at once*. Once again the action languished. Once again Mrs. Ritchie with some ladies of the Richmond committee descended on the Governor and Mr. Langfitt as they dined in a local hotel. To assure that the promises were kept they gathered in a body and filed into the gallery of the Virginia State House. When the House passed the bill, they then proceeded to the Senate. Their presence assured its victorious passage. But it was the first time that the Ladies had taken such a public stand.

Edward Everett's oration in Richmond coincided with the events of the Virginia Legislature. During the next three years he delivered his oration one hundred and twenty-nine times in every part of the country. He not only publicized what the Ladies of the Mount Vernon Association were endeavoring to do, he received additional contributions. His own fees and lectures were put into the hands of Boston businessmen who invested it, and increased it. With this and the fees for newspaper articles, he turned over to the Association $69,024, a little more than one-third of the whole price of Mount Vernon.

Meanwhile, there were more battles to be fought and won. Shortly after the success of chartering the Mount Vernon Association, John Augustine Washington withdrew the estate from sale. He believed that the charter as drawn represented a threat. He also doubted the ability of the ladies to raise the $200,000 price he had set. But Pamela Cunningham was ready to put her entire physical stamina and strength onto the altar of what had now become a holy cause. She wrote to Mr. Washington and proposed to come personally to

Mount Vernon. The event was Providential!

One must read the account given by Elswyth Thane in her memorable book *Mount Vernon is Ours: The Story of the Preservation and Restoration of George Washington's Home*. With intense suffering and the physical discomfort of the trip for one who was unable to walk or move, Miss Cunningham claimed in her heart *Mount Vernon is ours!!* She overcame every obstacle and personally met the Washingtons. But the cause seemed hopeless although both Mrs. Washington and John Augustine were moved by her impassioned pleas.

After a wretched night Miss Cunningham prepared to take the boat which stopped at the Mount Vernon landing — but it left without her. It was while she was waiting with the Washingtons for the next boat that Divine Providence unlocked the hard core of resistance. Ann Pamela Cunningham discovered the character assassination which had so wounded and belittled Mr. John Augustine Washington.

MOUNT VERNON LANDING
Sketch by Benson Lossing

As Miss Cunningham expressed her concern for Mr. Washington and indicated that the Mount Vernon Ladies were aware of the insulting treatment he had received, the dam of pent-up feelings and resentment burst. She learned from John Washington of his deep suspicions and wounds. She understood. As a southern woman, Miss Cunningham knew that a gentleman's honor had been impugned.

JOHN AUGUSTINE
WASHINGTON

I looked up to him as I said this. What a change in his face! Unawares, I had at last touched the sore spot, the obstacle no money could have removed.... I then told him if he would consent to overcome minor objections that I would prove to the country what were the feelings of the Association by going before the Legislature and asking it to make every change he required.... I held out my hand, he put his in mine. Then, with quivering lips, moist eyes, and a heart too full for him to speak, our compact was closed in silence...."[7]

Miss Cunningham declared that the awful journey home nearly killed her — but God alone knew the sacrifice, the mental and physical labor which the crusade for Mount Vernon personally cost her.

On April 6, 1858, John Augustine Washington set his hand to a contract of sale to the Mount Vernon Ladies' Association of the Union. "The terms were $18,000 down, an additional $57,000 the following December, and the balance in four equal annual installments. As a matter of fact all, except about $6,000 was paid in less than three years."[8]

Mount Vernon was Ours. Our national home has been preserved. But the Civil War burst upon the land and one more chapter had to be written before Ann Pamela Cunningham and the Ladies could begin their work of restoration. This chapter also has its

---

[7] Thane, *Mount Vernon is Ours*, p. 43.
[8] Johnson, *Mount Vernon: The Story of a Shrine*, pp. 21-22.

heroine — a unique woman of courage and determination — as she personally protected Mount Vernon by living on the premises for seven years during the dangers and threats of the War and in between two Armies. Only *"the presence of a lady" saved the day.*

Presence of a Lady

MOUNT VERNON, WEST FRONT
Sketch by Benson Lossing

If one lady had been successful in the purchase of Mount Vernon, another lady was to be called to special duty during the Civil War — to be present on the premises so that no harm would come to America's first home. This lady was Miss Sarah C. Tracy of Troy, New York.

Gift to Nelly Custis from George Washington

FIRST ORIGINAL FURNITURE RETURNED TO MOUNT VERNON

In 1853 Ann Pamela Cunningham began her work as Regent of the Mount Vernon Ladies' Association. She planned to take up residence at Mount Vernon as soon as the Washingtons moved out so that she could personally supervise the work of restoration. This work had already begun under the superintendence of Upton H. Herbert, a Virginian. Since Miss Cunningham was also a southerner, it was thought that she might give balance by engaging Miss Tracy of Troy, New York, as secretary.

But the Civil War interrupted everyone's plans. Miss Cunningham returned to South Carolina to protect her own property just when, in December of 1860, South Carolina seceded from the Union and she was unable to leave her plantation home. She would not be able to return to Mount Vernon for more than six years.

It was during the next seven years that Miss Tracy stayed at Mount Vernon, used by the Lord to protect America's national home by "the presence of a lady." It was important to maintain the neutrality of Mount Vernon so that the armies of both sides would respect the property. Mount Vernon was so close to the battle field that during the Battle of Bull Run the windows rattled from the thunder of the guns. Sometimes they could hear musket fire as small contingencies of cavalry fought in the neighborhood. Always there were "stragglers, deserters, escaped prisoners, and bushwackers" swarming about.

Miss Tracy was called upon to extraordinary service beyond any person's expectation. Mr. Herbert, despite his confederate sympathies and his desire to serve in the war, had promised to stay and manage the estate. He kept his promise at great personal cost and was confined to the property for he would have been arrested had he set foot in the city of Alexandria. Most of his southern friends wondered at his activities.

With a companion, Miss Mary McKim, for most of the years, Miss Sarah Tracy's activities for Mount Vernon included far more than the duties of a secretary. The war years were lean years and sums of money had to be raised for food and repairs. Miss Tracy, without much help from the few hired men left on the place, made bracelets from coffee beans, 800 small bouquets to sell to soldiers and visitors, had photographs taken. At times she took their garden produce to sell for "meat, salt, pepper — and on rare occasions, tea or coffee." We picture this small woman driving wagonloads of cabbages to market, avoiding roadblocks of soldiers, sometimes traveling alone, and at night, constantly aware of the presence of armed men. The Hand of the Lord protected her.

Mount Vernon residents were subject to chills and fevers from the nearby swamps and Miss Tracy nursed many — as well as herself. But in all the difficulties she radiated cheerfulness and optimism and never conveyed in her letters the quality of her courage or devotion. Without the quiet presence of Mr. Upton, and without her faith in the Lord, she would never have been able to carry on for those long seven years. She wrote to one friend:

MISS SARAH TRACY

> Thus you see we are once more quiet, I have climbed the 'Hill Difficulty' once more. I may find myself at the bottom again tomorrow, but I never anticipate. I have found the troubles of today so absorbing as to annihilate those of yesterday, and those of tomorrow too far off to command attention. I have so much to be thankful for. I have found that as the path of duty has been made plain to me, God, who is the strength of the weak and confiding, has gone beside me, smoothing the rough places; and where the help of human friend was needed, placing the kind and willing in my way.[9]

In 1868, just after New Year's Day, Miss Tracy left Mount Vernon in full confidence of Miss Cunningham's return. It was only much, much later, actually years later, that the Ladies of Mount Vernon realized the contribution which Sarah Tracy had made. Then they wanted the record, her *memoranda* of the period. But God had a special blessing for the faithful two of the Civil War. In 1872 Miss Tracy and Mr. Herbert were married, and a new life emerged from the terrible years as they lived out their days happily in Virginia.

In 1866, at the close of the War Between the States, Ann Pamela Cunningham, the Regent of the Mount Vernon Ladies' Association of the Union, met with her Council at Mount Vernon. There were many missing faces not able to be present at this historic meeting, but those who were there remember these words from the woman who had been inspired to make a reality of the goal of rescuing, preserving, and now of restoring Mount Vernon:

> Looking back from our present assured stand-point of an *accomplished fact*, my memory cannot fail to recall the early vicissitudes, the oft-discouraging progress of our labor of love in redeeming from oblivion and sure decay the home and grave of the immortal Washington! Then we lived on hope!

---

[9] Muir, *Presence of a Lady*, p. 56.

We *would* not yield to despair. Now we can rejoice, with intense satisfaction, to know that *Mount Vernon is ours* — the Nation's! And well may I feel almost overpowered to find myself, at this moment, in the midst of ladies representing the varied sections of our country, pledged to guard that sacred spot *forever*....[10]

Mount Vernon is open to the public every day in the year, from 9 o'clock.

MOUNT VERNON LADIES ASSOCIATION 1870 COUNCIL
(from left, standing) Mrs. Barry, Mrs. Walker, Mrs. Washington, Mrs. Halsted, Mrs. Emory, Mrs. Chace;
(seated) Mrs. Mitchell, Mrs. Brooks, Mrs. Sweat, Miss Cunningham, Mrs. Comegys, Mrs. Eve

As Elswyth Thane writes:

It takes only a dozen words to encompass the achievement of a little miracle. But in that simple statement resides a great dream come true, accomplished by more than a hundred years of dedicated effort by an organization of remarkable women, assembled one by one from nearly every state in the union.[11]

America's "falling away" period began some fifty years after the establishment of the Constitution of the United States. As we became indifferent to our Biblical principles of character and government, this was reflected in our indifference to our ancient landmarks. It is not surprising that we neglected to care for and cherish the home of the man God raised up to lead the Continental Army and to establish the American Presidency. Yet, even in our period of decline, God had his remnant. Steps were taken, initiated by the women of America. This is a story which we need to take into our hearts and to record as a unique contribution of our American Christian women. Mount Vernon has been preserved for us — but each generation will need to continue to support and maintain it for future generations.

Let us heed Scripture's admonition: *"If the foundations be destroyed, what can the righteous do."* (Psalms 11:3) The "righteous" can rebuild them.

---

[10] Thane, *Mount Vernon is Ours*, p. xi.
[11] *Ibid.*, p. 3.

THE MOUNT VERNON LADIES' ASSOCIATION OF THE UNION

A fine source of books about our heroines and also about George Washington himself can be obtained from Mount Vernon Ladies' Association, Mail Order Department, Mount Vernon, Virginia 22121. They will send, upon request, lists of literature, reproductions, slides, films, and other miscellaneous items. Especially recommended are the following books:

Presence of a Lady: Mount Vernon 1861–1868, by Dorothy Troth Muir

Mount Vernon: The Story of a Shrine, by Gerald W. Johnson and Charles Cecil Wall

Maxims of Washington, Political, Social, Moral, and Religious

Washington's Lady, The Life of Martha Washington, by Elswyth Thane, Dodd, Mead & Company, 1960 (Not a Christian biography, but well done.)

Potomac Squire, by Elswyth Thane, Mount Vernon Ladies' Association, 1963. Excellent biography of George Washington, revealing his great love for Mount Vernon through the many letters he wrote and his work in building his home.

Mount Vernon Family, by Elswyth Thane, Crowell-Collier Press, 1968. A chronicle of the young people who looked to our first President for love, guidance, and support.

Mount Vernon is Ours, The Story of the Preservation and Restoration of Washington's Home, by Elswyth Thane, Duell, Soan and Pearce, 1966.

Many of these books can be found in your public library. If you search, perhaps you can obtain the books by Elswyth Thane from secondhand book stores or through a good book service able to search out these titles for you.

MOUNT VERNON
Sketch by Benson Lossing

The Charter Oak

In 1662, King Charles II of England granted a charter to the Connecticut colony. Charles was succeeded by his brother, James. Immediately on the accession of James, they arranged a plan for procuring a surrender of all the patents of the New England colonies. The colony of Connecticut sent an agent to England with a petition and remonstrances to the king. The mission was in vain, for already the decree had gone forth for annulling the charters. Sir Edmund Andross was appointed the first governor general, and arrived at Boston in December, 1686. He immediately demanded the surrender of the charter of Connecticut, and it was refused. In October, 1687, he went to Hartford with a company of soldiers while the Assembly was in session, and demanded an immediate surrender of their charter. The charter was brought forth and placed upon the table around which the members were sitting. Andross was about to seize it, when the lights were suddenly extinguished. The moment the lights disappeared several people entered the chamber. Captain Wadsworth of Hartford seized the charter, and, unobserved, carried it off and deposited it in the hollow trunk of a large oak-tree. The candles were relighted, but the coveted parchment was gone.

The opening of the cavity wherein the charter was concealed is seen near the roots. The trunk was twenty-five feet in circumference. It is said that the cavity which was the asylum of the charter was large enough to admit a child. Within the space of eight years that cavity had closed, as if it had fulfilled its divine purpose.

The Charter Oak appears here as it did in 1848, when this sketch was made by Benson Lossing.

TITLE INDEX

To update the information below, check the current edition of *Books in Print* by R.R. Bowker through your local bookstore or library.

KEY: OP (out-of-print); FACE (order from FACE); *FACE (with Teaching Syllabus from Rosalie Slater)

Title	Order From, or Out-of-Print
Abe Lincoln Grows Up by Carl Sandburg	FACE
Abraham Lincoln by Ingri and Edgar Parin d'Aulaire	FACE
Abraham Lincoln: God's Leader for a Nation by David Collins	FACE
Abraham Lincoln: The Man and His Faith by G. Frederick Owen	TYNDALE
Admiral of the Ocean Sea: A Life of Christopher Columbus by Samuel Eliot Morison	LITTLE
Admiral Richard E. Byrd by Alfred Steinberg	PUTNAM
Adventures of Captain Bonneville, USA by Washington Irving	U. OF OK
All About Horses by Marguerite Henry	OP
Alone by Admiral Richard E. Byrd	PUTNAM
American Dictionary of the English Language (1828) by Noah Webster	FACE
American History in Verse by Burton Egbert Stevenson	BOB JONES
Amos Fortune, Free Man by Elizabeth Yates	PENGUIN
Annotated Mother Goose by William S. and Ceil Barring-Gould	PENGUIN
Antarctica by Emil Schulthess	SIMON
"Antarctica: Seeking the Biblical Purpose...," *Journal I* by Rosalie Slater	FACE
Astoria by Washington Irving	GORDON
Autobiography of Benjamin Franklin	HOUGHTON; MACMILLAN; PENGUIN
Ben Hur: A Tale of the Christ by Lew Wallace	FACE
Ben Hur: A Tale of the Christ – Teacher's Guide	OP
Benjamin Franklin by Ingri and Edgar Parin d'Aulaire	FACE
Benjamin West and His Cat Grimalkin by Marguerite Henry	*FACE
Big Snow, The by Berta and Elmer Hader	MACMILLAN
Biography of Cyrus Field (Atlantic Cable) by Jean Lee Latham	OP
Biography of Washington Irving by Professor Stanley Williams	OXFORD U.
Bird's Christmas Carol, The by Kate Douglas Wiggin	OP
Black Gold by Marguerite Henry	MACMILLAN
Blue Willow by Doris Gates	FACE
Book of Abigail and John: Selected Letters... by John & Abigail Adams	HARVARD
Book of Life, Newton Hall & Irving Wood, ed. (early editions)	OP
Book of Nursery and Mother Goose Rhymes by Marguerite de Angeli	FACE
Born to Trot by Marguerite Henry	MACMILLAN
Bright April by Marguerite de Angeli	OP
Brighty of the Grand Canyon by Marguerite Henry	MACMILLAN
Butterflies Come, The by Leo Politi	OP
Captain John Smith's America ed. by John Lankford	HARPER
Carry On, Mr. Bowditch by Jean Lee Latham	*FACE
"Character of Washington" (speech) by Edward Everett (see Thane, *Mt. Vernon is Ours*)	
Charles Dickens: His Tragedy and Triumph by Edgar Johnson	SIMON
Children and Books by May Hill Arbuthnot	SCOTT
Child's Book of Poems illus. by Gyo Fujikawa	FACE
Child's Garden of Verses, A, by Robert Louis Stevenson	FACE
Child's History of England by Charles Dickens	OP
Child's Journey with Dickens by Kate Douglas Wiggin	OP
Christian History of the Constitution Series, by Verna M. Hall VOL. I, *Christian Self-Government*; & VOL. II, *Christian Self-Government with Union*	FACE
Christian History of the American Revolution: Consider and Ponder by Verna M. Hall	FACE
Christian Home, The by Rev. S. Phillips (see *Teaching & Learning*, FACE)	
Christmas Books by Charles Dickens	OP
Christmas Carol, A by Charles Dickens	FACE
Christopher Columbus & the Discovery of the New World by J. Pollard	OP
Cinnabar: The One O'Clock Fox by Marguerite Henry	MACMILLAN
Columbus's Book of Prophecies by Kay Brigham	CLIE
Columbus by Ingri and Edgar Parin d'Aulaire	FACE
Courage of Sarah Noble, The by Alice Dalgliesh	MACMILLAN
Courage of Sarah Noble, Teacher (reading comp. workbook)	MILE-HI
Crossing of Antarctica: Commonwealth Trans-Arctic Expedition 1955–1958 by Vivian and Sir Edmund Hillary Fuchs	LITTLE
Dancing Cloud by Mary and Conrad Buff	OP
David Copperfield, The Personal History of, by Charles Dickens	OXFORD U.

Title	Order From, or Out-of-Print
David Brainard: Missionary to the Indians (biog.) by Jonathan Edwards	OP
Dear Marguerite Henry, orig. *Dear Readers & Riders* by Marguerite Henry	OP
Deerslayer, or The First War Path by James Fenimore Cooper	*FACE
Dickens' Works edited by Eleanor Farjeon (look for other editions)	OP
Discovery by Admiral Richard E. Byrd	AYER
Divine Songs in Easy Language for the Use of Children by Isaac Watts	CUMBERLAND
European Discovery of America (2 vols.) by Samuel Eliot Morison	OXFORD U.
Eddie Rickenbacker: Young Racer and Flyer by Catherine Cleven	OP
Edward Rickenbacker, An Autobiography	PRENTICE
Everyday Life in Bible Times	NAT'L. GEOG.
Family Study on...George Washington... by Belinda Beth Ballenger	N.WEB.
Five Little Peppers and How They Grew by Margaret Sidney	PUTNAM
Five O'Clock Charlie by Marguerite Henry	MACMILLAN
Flip, the Story of a Flying Horse by Wesley Dennis	OP
French and American Revolutions Compared, The by Gentz (see *Three Revolutions*)	
From Father to Son: Letters of Captain Eddie Rickenbacker...	WALKER
George Washington by Ingri and Edgar Parin d'Aulaire	FACE
Gingerbread Boy, The by Paul Galdone	HOUGHTON
Glory and the Dream: Abraham Lincoln by Michael A. Musmanno	LONG HOUSE
Good News from Virginia by Edward Winslow	OP
Grandfather's Chair: True Stories from New England's History by Nathaniel Hawthorne	OP
Great Expectations by Charles Dickens	FACE
Greek Treasure, Biog. Novel of Henry & Sophia Schliemann by Irving Stone	BANTAM
Group, The, a play, by Mercy Warren (see *Consider and Ponder*, FACE)	
Hah-Nee by Mary and Conrad Buff	OP
Hall, Verna M., Biog.: "Partners of a Glorious Hope," Journal, Vol. I	FACE
Helen Keller by Margaret Davidson	SCHOLASTIC
Helen Keller, The Story of My Life (autobiography)	FACE
Henner's Lydia by Marguerite de Angeli	OP
History 'Of Plimoth Plantation' by William Bradford (see *Christian History* VOL. I, FACE)	
History of the...American Revolution by Mercy Warren (see *Consider and Ponder*, FACE)	
History of the Reign of Ferdinand & Isabella the Catholic (1890) by William H. Prescott	OP
History of the United States, VOL. I-II, by David Ramsey (see *Consider and Ponder*, FACE)	
Home Book of Verse for Young Folks by Burton Egbert Stevenson	HOLD
House of the Seven Gables, The by Nathaniel Hawthorne	FACE
In My Mother's House by Ann Nolan Clark, illus. by Herrera	OP
Introducing Charles Dickens by May Lamberton Becker	DODD
Invincible Louisa by Cornelia Meigs	LITTLE
Island of the Blue Dolphins by Scott O'Dell	HOUGHTON
Ivanhoe by Sir Walter Scott	*FACE
Joel: A Boy of Galilee by Annie Fellows Johnston	FACE
John Paul Jones: A Sailor's Biography by Samuel Eliot Morison	U. OF NEBRASKA
John Smith, Man of Adventure by Miriam E. Mason	HOUGHTON
Journals of Washington Irving	HASKELL
Justin Morgan Had a Horse by Marguerite Henry	FACE
Juanita by Leo Politi	OP
Kate Douglas Wiggin, As Her Sister Knew Her by Nora Archibald Smith	WEST, R.
King of the Wind: Story of the Godolphin Arabian by Marguerite Henry	MACMILLAN
Knickerbocker's History of New York by Washington Irving	OP
Lamb, The (poem) by William Blake (see *Oxford Book of Children's Verse*)	
Last Hero: Charles A. Lindbergh, The by Walter S. Ross	HARPER
Last of the Mohicans by James Fenimore Cooper	MACMILLAN
Laura (Biog. of Laura Ingalls Wilder) by Donald Zochert	HARPER
Lay of the Last Minstrel (poem) by Sir Walter Scott	OP
Legend of Sleepy Hollow & Other Stories by Washington Irving	FACE
Lew Wallace: Boy Writer by Martha Schaaf	OP

115

Title	Order From, or Out-of-Print
Lew Wallace: Militant Romantic by Robert & Katherine Morseberger	MCGRAW-HILL
Life and Epistles of St. Paul (1869) by Revs. W.J. Conybeare & J.S. Howson	OP
Life and Letters of Washington Irving by Pierre M. Irving	OP
Life and Voyages of Columbus by Washington Irving	A.M.S.
Life of George Washington in Words of One Syllable by Josephine Pollard	MILE-HI
Life of Our Lord, The by Charles Dickens	OP
Life of Washington (in two volumes) by Washington Irving	OP
Little America by Admiral Richard E. Byrd	OP
Little Colonel Series, The by Annie Fellows Johnston	ZENGER
Little Engine That Could, The by Watty Piper	PUTNAM
Little Fellow by Marguerite Henry	OP
Little House, The by Virginia Lee Burton	HOUGHTON
Little House in the Big Woods by Laura Ingalls Wilder	*FACE
Little Navajo Bluebird by Ann Nolan Clark	OP
Little Toot by Hardie Gramatky	PUTNAM
Little Women by Louisa Alcott	*FACE
Make Way for the Ducklings by Robert McCloskey	PENGUIN
Making of George Washington, Patriotic Ed. by Gen. William H. Wilbur	FACE
Man Who Dared the Lightning, The by Thomas J. Fleming	MORROW
Marco Polo by Gian Paolo Ceserani	PUTNAM
Maria: The Potter of San Idlefonso by Alice Marriott	U. OF OK
Matchlock Gun, The by Walter D. Edmonds	DODD
Matthew Fontaine Maury: Scientist of the Sea by Frances Williams	RUTGERS U.
Maybelle, The Cable Car by Virginia Lee Burton	OP
Meet Abraham Lincoln by Barbara Cary	RANDOM
Meet Benjamin Franklin by Maggi Scarf	RANDOM
Meet George Washington by Joan Heilbroner	RANDOM
Men Under the Sea by Commander Ellsberg	OP
Mike Mulligan and His Steam Shovel by Virginia Lee Burton	HOUGHTON
Millions of Cats by Wanda Gag	PUTNAM
Misty of Chincoteague by Marguerite Henry	FACE
Moby Dick by Herman Melville	FACE
Mother Carey's Chickens by Kate Douglas Wiggin	FACE
Mount Vernon Family by Elswyth Thane	MT. VERNON
Mount Vernon is Ours: Preservation…of Washington's Home by Elswyth Thane	MT. VERNON
Mount Vernon: Story of a Shrine by Gerald Johnson & Charles Wall	MT. VERNON
Mustang: Wild Spirit of the West by Marguerite Henry	FACE
My Little Sister, Marguerite Henry by Gertrude Jupp	OP
Narcissa Whitman: Pioneer of Oregon by Jeanette Eaton	HARCOURT
Narrative of the Captivity & Restoration of Mrs. Mary Rowlandson	OP
Noah Webster: Father of the Dictionary by Isabel Proudfit	*FACE
Noah Webster: Master of Words by David Collins	*FACE
Ocean Gold by Commander Ellsberg	OP
Ocean Pathfinder: Biog. of…Maury by Frances Williams	HARCOURT
On Heroes, Hero-Worship and the Heroic in History by Thomas Carlyle	U. OF NEBRASKA
One Man's Horse by Marguerite Henry	OP
Oxford Book of Children's Verse by Iona and Peter Opie	OXFORD U.
Oxford Nursery Rhyme Book by Iona and Peter Opie	OXFORD U.
Pathfinder of the Seas: Life of…Maury by John Wayland	OP
Pedro, the Angel of Olvera Street by Leo Politi	OP
Pelle's New Suit by Elsa Beskow	HARPER
Peter Lundy and the Medicine Hat Stallion by Marguerite Henry	OP
Phillis Wheatley: America's First Black Poetess by Miriam Morris Fuller	GARRARD
Physical Geography by Arnold Guyot	ACHI
Physical Geography of the Sea and Its Meteorology by Matthew Fontaine Maury	HARVARD U.
Pilgrim's Progress by John Bunyan	FACE
Pocahontas by Grace Steele Woodward	FACE
Pocahontas by Ingri and Edgar Parin d'Aulaire	FACE
Poems of Phillis Wheatley ed. by Julian D. Macon, Jr.	U. OF NC
Potomac Squire by Elswyth Thane	MT. VERNON
Presence of a Lady: Mount Vernon 1861–1868 by Dorothy Troth Muir	MT. VERNON
Prince Henry the Navigator & Highways of the Sea by Thomas Caldecot Chubb	OP
Quentin Durwood by Sir Walter Scott	AIRMONT
Read-Aloud Handbook by Jim Trelease	PENGUIN
Rebecca of Sunnybrook Farm by Kate Douglas Wiggin (Airmont)	FACE
"Reflections on the Russian Revolution," by Stefan T. Possony *Three Revolutions*	OP
Rights of the Br. Colonies Asserted & Proved, by James Otis (see *Christian History*, VOL. II, FACE)	
Rip Van Winkle & the Legend of Sleepy Hollow by Washington Irving	SLEEPY HOLLOW RES.
Rise of the Republic of the U.S. by Richard Frothingham (see *Christian History* VOL. I, FACE)	
Riverside Magazine for Young People, Horace Elisha Scudder, ed.	OP
Robert Fulton, Boy Craftsman by Marguerite Henry	MILE-HI
Robert Louis Stevenson: Storyteller & Adventurer by Katharine Wilkie	HOUGHTON
Runnaway Bunny, The by Margaret Wise Brown	HARPER
Samuel F. B. Morse by Jean Lee Latham	OP
Scarlet Letter, The by Nathaniel Hawthorne	FACE
Scarlet Pimpernel, The by Baroness Orczy	AIRMONT
Sea Star: Orphan of Chincoteague by Marguerite Henry	MACMILLAN
Sir Walter Scott: the Great Unknown by Edgar Johnson	MACMILLAN
Sir Walter Scott: Wizard of the North by Pearle Henriksen Schultz	*FACE
Sketch Book of Geoffrey Crayon, Gentleman by Washington Irving	FACE
Skyward by Admiral Richard E. Byrd	OP
Song of the Swallows by Leo Politi	MACMILLAN
Spirit of St. Louis by Charles A. Lindbergh	*FACE
Stormy: Misty's Foal by Marguerite Henry	MACMILLAN
Story About Ping by Majorie and Kurt Wiese Flack	PENGUIN
Swiss Family Robinson, The by J. R. Wyss	PUTNAM
Tale of Peter Rabbit and Other Stories by Beatrix Potter	PENGUIN
Tale of Two Cities by Charles Dickens	FACE
Tales of a Grandfather, Being Stories from the History of Scotland by Sir Walter Scott	OP
Tales of the Alhambra by Washington Irving	RANDOM
Talisman, The by Sir Walter Scott	BIBLIO
Tanglewood Tales by Nathaniel Hawthorne	AIRMONT
Teaching and Learning America's Christian History: The Principle Approach by Rosalie J. Slater	FACE
"Teaching Elem. Students…Alone," by Linda Andrus, *Journal I*	FACE
Tenth Muse, Lately Sprung Up in America: Poems of Anne Bradstreet, 1870	OP
Thee Hannah by Marguerite de Angeli	DOUBLEDAY
Thirty Fathoms Deep by Commander Ellsberg	OP
Thread That Runs So True: Story of a Kentucky Mountain School-Teacher by Jesse Stuart	FACE
Three Revolutions… by Gentz (tr. Adams) & Possony	OP
Three Worlds of Captain John Smith by Philip L. Barbour	HOUGHTON
Time of Wonder by Robert McCloskey	PENGUIN
To Young Women by Lydia Sigourney (see *Christian History*, VOL. I, FACE)	
Tour on the Prairies by Washington Irving	U. OF OK
Travels of Marco Polo	FACE
Treasure Island by Robert Louis Stevenson	FACE
Up the Hill by Marguerite de Angeli	OP
Velveteen Rabbit, The by Margery Williams	BANTAM
Walls of Windy Troy: Biography of Heinrich Schliemann by Marjorie Braymer	HARCOURT
Wartime Journals of Charles A. Lindbergh	HARCOURT
Washington's Lady: Life of Martha Washington by Elswyth Thane	MT. VERNON
Waterless Mountain by Laura Adams Armer	RANDOM
Where the Wild Things Are by Maurice Sendak	HARPER
White Stallion of Lipazza by Marguerite Henry	MACMILLAN
Wildest Horse Race in the World by Marguerite Henry	MACMILLAN
Women of the American Revolution by Elizabeth Ellet (see *Consider and Ponder*, FACE)	
Wonder Book, A by Nathaniel Hawthorne	FACE
Works of Anne Bradstreet, The Jeannine Hensley, ed.	FACE
Writings of Kate Douglas Wiggin: A Child's Journey with Dickens	OP
Yearling, The by Marjorie Kinnan Rawlings	MACMILLAN

AUTHOR INDEX

To update the information below, check the current edition of *Books in Print* by R.R. Bowker through your local bookstore or library.

KEY: OP (out-of-print); FACE (order from FACE); *FACE (with Teaching Syllabus; see titles below)

	Order From, or Out-of-Print
Adams, John and Abigail Adams	
Book of Abigail and John: Selected Letters of the Adams Family	HARVARD
Adams, John Quincy, Translator	
"French & American Revolutions...by Gentz," *Three Revolutions*	OP
Alcott, Louisa	
Little Women	*FACE
Alcott, Louisa, Biography of:	
Invincible Louisa by Cornelia Meigs	LITTLE
Arbuthnot, May Hill	
Children and Books	SCOTT
Armer, Laura Adams	
Waterless Mountain	RANDOM
Ballenger, Belinda Beth	
Family Study on the Life of George Washington...	N.WEB.
Barbour, Philip L.	
Three Worlds of Captain John Smith	HOUGHTON
Barring-Gould, William S. and Ceil	
Annotated Mother Goose	PENGUIN
Becker, May Lamberton	
Introducing Charles Dickens	DODD
Beskow, Elsa	
Pelle's New Suit	HARPER
Blake, William	
The Lamb (poem), see *Oxford Book of Children's Verse*	
Bradford, William	
History 'Of Plimoth Plantation' (see *Christian History* VOL. I, FACE)	
Bradstreet, Anne	
Tenth Muse, Lately Sprung Up in America: Poems of Anne Bradstreet, 1870	OP
Works of Anne Bradstreet, The Jeannine Hensley, ed.	FACE
Braymer, Marjorie	
Walls of Windy Troy: Biography of Heinrich Schliemann	HARCOURT
Brigham, Kay	
Columbus's Book of Prophecies (and related biography)	LIBROS CLIE
Brown, Margaret Wise	
The Runaway Bunny	HARPER
Buff, Mary and Conrad	
Dancing Cloud	OP
Hah-Nee	OP
Bunyan, John	
Pilgrim's Progress	FACE
Burton, Virginia Lee	
Little House, The	HOUGHTON
Maybelle, The Cable Car	OP
Mike Mulligan and His Steam Shovel	HOUGHTON
Byrd, Admiral Richard E.	
Alone	PUTNAM
Discovery	AYER
Little America	OP
Skyward	OP
Byrd, Admiral Richard E., Biographies of:	
Admiral Richard E. Byrd by Alfred Steinberg	PUTNAM
"Teaching Elem. Students...*Alone,*" by Linda Andrus, *Journal 1*	FACE
Carlyle, Thomas	
On Heroes, Hero-Worship and the Heroic in History	U. OF NEBRASKA
Cary, Barbara	
Meet Abraham Lincoln	RANDOM
Ceserani, Gian Paolo	
Marco Polo	PUTNAM
Chubb, Thomas Caldecot	
Prince Henry the Navigator and the Highways of the Sea	OP
Clark, Ann Nolan	
In My Mother's House illus. by Herrera	OP
Litttle Navajo Bluebird	OP
Cleven, Catherine	
Eddie Rickenbacker: Young Racer and Flyer	OP
Collins, David	
Abraham Lincoln: God's Leader for a Nation	FACE
Noah Webster: Master of Words	*FACE

	Order From, or Out-of-Print
Conybeare, Rev. W. J. and Rev. J. S. Howson	
Life and Epistles of Saint Paul, 1869	OP
Cooper, James Fenimore	
Deerslayer, or The First War Path	*FACE
Last of the Mohicans	MACMILLAN
d'Aulaire, Ingri and Edgar Parin	
Abraham Lincoln	FACE
Benjamin Franklin	FACE
Columbus	FACE
George Washington	FACE
Pocahontas	FACE
Dalgliesh, Alice	
Courage of Sarah Noble	MACMILLAN
Courage of Sarah Noble, Teacher (reading comp. workbook)	MILE-HI
Davidson, Margaret	
Helen Keller	SCHOLASTIC
de Angeli, Marguerite	
Book of Nursery and Mother Goose Rhymes	FACE
Thee Hannah	DOUBLEDAY
Henner's Lydia	OP
Up the Hill	OP
Bright April	OP
Dennis, Wesley	
Flip, the Story of a Flying Horse	OP
Dickens, Charles	
Child's History of England	OP
Christmas Books	OP
Christmas Carol, A	FACE
Dickens' Works edited by Eleanor Farjeon (look for other editions)	OP
Great Expectations	FACE
Life of Our Lord, The	OP
Personal History of David Copperfield (in collection)	OXFORD U.
Tale of Two Cities	FACE
Dickens, Charles, Biographies of:	
Charles Dickens: His Tragedy and Triumph by Edgar Johnson	SIMON
Child's Journey with Dickens by Kate Douglas Wiggin	OP
Introducing Charles Dickens by May Lamberton Becker	DODD
Eaton, Jeanette	
Narcissa Whitman: Pioneer of Oregon	HARCOURT
Edmonds, Walter D.	
The Matchlock Gun	DODD
Edwards, Jonathan	
Biog. of David Brainard: Missionary to the Indians	OP
Ellet, Elizabeth	
Women of the American Revolution (see *Consider and Ponder,* FACE)	
Ellsberg, Commander	
Men Under the Sea	OP
Ocean Gold	OP
Thirty Fathoms Deep	OP
Everett, Edward	
"Character of Washington" (speech), (see Thane, *Mt. Vernon is Ours*)	
Flack, Majorie and Kurt Wiese	
Story About Ping	PENGUIN
Fleming, Thomas J.	
Man Who Dared the Lightning, The	MORROW
Franklin, Benjamin	
Autobiography of Benjamin Franklin	HOUGHTON; MACMILLAN; PENGUIN
Franklin, Benjamin, Biographies of:	
Benjamin Franklin by Ingri and Edgar Parin d'Aulaire	FACE
Man Who Dared the Lightning, The by Thomas J. Fleming	MORROW
Meet Benjamin Franklin by Maggi Scarf	RANDOM
Frothingham, Richard	
Rise of the Republic of the U.S., 1890 (see *Christian History* VOL. I, FACE)	
Fuchs, Vivian and Sir Edmund Hillary	
Crossing of Antarctica: Commonwealth Trans-Arctic Exp. 1955–1958	LITTLE
Fujikawa, Gyo, illustrator	
Child's Book of Poems	FACE
Fuller, Miriam Morris	
Phillis Wheatley: America's First Black Poetess	GARRARD

	Order From, or Out-of-Print
Gag, Wanda	
Millions of Cats	PUTNAM
Galdone, Paul	
Gingerbread Boy, The	HOUGHTON
Gates, Doris	
Blue Willow	FACE
Gentz, Friedrich	
"French and American Revolutions Compared," *Three Revolutions*	OP
Gramatky, Hardie	
Little Toot	PUTNAM
Grosvenor, Melville Bell, Foreward	
Everyday Life in Bible Times, NAT'L. GEOG.	OP
Guyot, Arnold	
Physical Geography	ACHI
Hader, Berta and Elmer	
The Big Snow	MACMILLAN
Hall, Verna M. (FACE)	
Christian History of the Constitution: Christian Self-Government, VOL. I	FACE
Christian History . . . : Christian Self-Government with Union, VOL. II	FACE
Christian History of the American Revolution: Consider and Ponder	FACE
Hall, Verna M., Biography of:	
"Partners of a Glorious Hope," *The Journal,* VOL. I	FACE
Hawthorne, Nathaniel	
Grandfather's Chair: True Stories from New England's History	OP
House of the Seven Gables, The	FACE
Scarlet Letter, The	FACE
Tanglewood Tales	AIRMONT
Wonder Book, A	FACE
Heilbroner, Joan	
Meet George Washington	RANDOM
Henry, Marguerite	
All About Horses	OP
Benjamin West and His Cat Grimalkin	*FACE
Black Gold	MACMILLAN
Born to Trot	MACMILLAN
Brighty of the Grand Canyon	MACMILLAN
Cinnabar: The One O'Clock Fox	MACMILLAN
Dear Marguerite Henry, originally *Dear Readers and Riders*	OP
Five O'Clock Charlie	MACMILLAN
Justin Morgan Had a Horse	FACE
King of the Wind: Story of the Godolphin Arabian	MACMILLAN
Little Fellow	OP
Misty of Chincoteague	FACE
Mustang: Wild Spirit of the West	FACE
One Man's Horse	OP
Peter Lundy and the Medicine Hat Stallion	OP
Robert Fulton, Boy Craftsman	MILE-HI
Sea Star: Orphan of Chincoteague	MACMILLAN
Stormy: Misty's Foal	MACMILLAN
White Stallion of Lipazza	MACMILLAN
Wildest Horse Race in the World	MACMILLAN
Henry, Marguerite, Biography of:	
My Little Sister, Marguerite Henry by Gertrude Jupp	OP
Irving, Washington	
Adventures of Captain Bonneville, USA	U. OF OK.
Astoria	GORDON
Journals of Washington Irving	HASKELL
Knickerbocker's History of New York	OP
Legend of Sleepy Hollow & Other Stories	FACE
Life and Voyages of Columbus	A.M.S.
Life of Washington (in two volumes)	OP
Rip Van Winkle and the Legend of Sleepy Hollow	SLEEPY HOLLOW RES.
Sketch Book of Geoffrey Crayon, Gentleman	FACE
Tales of the Alhambra	RANDOM
Tour on the Prairies	U. OF OK
Irving, Washington, Biographies of:	
Biography of Washington Irving by Professor Stanley Williams	OXFORD U.
Life and Letters of Washington Irving by Pierre M. Irving	OP
Johnson, Edgar	
Charles Dickens: His Tragedy and Triumph	SIMON
Sir Walter Scott: the Great Unknown	MACMILLAN
Johnson, Gerald W. and Charles Cecil Wall	
Mount Vernon: Story of a Shrine	MT. VERNON

	Order From, or Out-of-Print
Johnston, Annie Fellows	
Joel: A Boy of Galilee	FACE
The Little Colonel Series	ZENGER
Keller, Helen	
Helen Keller, The Story of My Life (autobiography)	FACE
Keller, Helen, Biographies of:	
Helen Keller by Margaret Davidson	SCHOLASTIC
Lankford, John, ed.	
Captain John Smith's America	HARPER
Latham, Jean Lee	
Biography of Cyrus Field (Atlantic Cable)	OP
Carry On, Mr. Bowditch	*FACE
Samuel F. B. Morse	OP
Lindbergh, Charles A.	
Spirit of St. Louis	*FACE
Wartime Journals of Charles A. Lindbergh	HARCOURT
Lindbergh, Charles A., Biography of:	
Last Hero: Charles A. Lindbergh, The by Walter S. Ross	HARPER
Marriott, Alice	
Maria: The Potter of San Idlefonso	U. OF OK
Mason, Miriam E.	
John Smith, Man of Adventure	HOUGHTON
Maury, Matthew Fontaine	
Physical Geography of the Sea and Its Meteorology	HARVARD U.
Maury, Matthew Fontaine, Biographies of:	
Matthew Fontaine Maury: Scientist of the Sea by Frances Williams	RUTGERS U.
Ocean Pathfinder: Biog. of...Maury by Frances Williams	HARCOURT
Pathfinder of the Seas: Life of...Maury by John Wayland	OP
McCloskey, Robert	
Make Way for the Ducklings	PENGUIN
Time of Wonder	PENGUIN
Meigs, Cornelia	
Invincible Louisa	LITTLE
Melville, Herman	
Moby Dick	FACE
Morison, Samuel Eliot	
Admiral of the Ocean Sea: A Life of Christopher Columbus	LITTLE
European Discovery of America (2 vols.)	OXFORD U.
John Paul Jones: A Sailor's Biography	U. OF NEBRASKA
Musmanno, Michael A.	
Glory and the Dream: Abraham Lincoln...	LONG HOUSE
Muir, Dorothy Troth	
Presence of a Lady: Mount Vernon 1861–1868	MT. VERNON
O'Dell, Scott	
Island of the Blue Dolphins	HOUGHTON
Opie, Iona and Peter	
Oxford Book of Children's Verse	OXFORD U.
Oxford Nursery Rhyme Book	OXFORD U.
Orczy, Baroness	
The Scarlet Pimpernel	AIRMONT
Otis, James	
Rights of the Br. Colonies Asserted & Proved, (see *Christian History,* VOL. II, FACE)	
Owen, G. Frederick	
Abraham Lincoln: The Man and His Faith	TYNDALE
Phillips, Rev. S.	
The Christian Home (see *Teaching & Learning* pp. 4-37, FACE)	
Piper, Watty	
Little Engine That Could, The	PUTNAM
Politi, Leo	
Butterflies Come, The	OP
Juanita	OP
Pedro, the Angel of Olvera Street	OP
Song of the Swallows	MACMILLAN
Pollard, Josephine	
Christopher Columbus and the Discovery of the New World	OP
Life of George Washington in Words of One Syllable	MILE-HI
Polo, Marco	
Travels of Marco Polo	FACE
Potter, Beatrix	
Tale of Peter Rabbit and Other Stories, Warne	PENGUIN
Possony, Stefan T.	
"Reflections on the Russian Revolution," *Three Revolutions*	OP

	Order From, or Out-of-Print
Prescott, William H.	
History of the Reign of Ferdinand & Isabella the Catholic, 1890	OP
Proudfit, Isabel	
Noah Webster: Father of the Dictionary	*FACE
Ramsey, David	
History of the United States, VOL. I-II (see *Consider and Ponder,* FACE)	
Rawlings, Marjorie Kinnan	
The Yearling	MACMILLAN
Rickenbacker, Edward V.	
Edward Rickenbacker, An Autobiography	PRENTICE
From Father to Son: Letters of Captain Eddie Rickenbacker…	WALKER
Rickenbacker, Edward, Biography of:	
Eddie Rickenbacker: Young Racer and Flyer by Catherine Cleven	OP
Ross, Walter S.	
Last Hero: Charles A. Lindbergh	HARPER
Rowlandson, Mrs. Mary	
Narrative of the Captivity and Restoration of Mrs. Mary Rowlandson	OP
Sandburg, Carl	
Abe Lincoln Grows Up	FACE
Scarf, Maggi	
Meet Benjamin Franklin	RANDOM
Schulthess, Emil	
Antarctica	SIMON
Scott, Sir Walter	
Ivanhoe	*FACE
Lay of the Last Minstrel (poem)	OP
Quentin Durwood	AIRMONT
Tales of a Grandfather, Being Stories from the History of Scotland	OP
Talisman, The	BIBLIO
Scott, Sir Walter, Biographies of:	
Sir Walter Scott: the Great Unknown by Edgar Johnson	MACMILLAN
Sir Walter Scott: Wizard of the North by Pearle Henriksen Schultz	*FACE
Schultz, Pearle Henriksen	
Sir Walter Scott: Wizard of the North	*FACE
Scudder, Horace Elisha, ed.	
Riverside Magazine for Young People	OP
Sendak, Maurice	
Where the Wild Things Are	HARPER
Sidney, Margaret	
Five Little Peppers and How They Grew	PUTNAM
Sigourney, Lydia	
To Young Women (see *Christian History,* VOL. I, FACE)	
Slater, Rosalie J. (FACE)	
"Antarctica: Seeking the Biblical Purpose…," *Journal I*	FACE
Teaching and Learning America's Christian History:	
The Principle Approach	FACE
Teaching Syllabi for Key Classics:	
"American Men of Science and Invention" *Carry On, Mr. Bowditch*	*FACE
"American Character in Education" *Noah Webster:*	
Father of the Dictionary	*FACE
"Anglo-Saxon, Anglo-Norman Periods and Sir Walter Scott"	
Ivanhoe & Sir Walter Scott	*FACE
"Junior High Syllabus"	*FACE
"English Chivalry and Constitutional Seeds of Liberty" *Men of Iron*	*FACE
"Extending Pilgrim-Pioneer Character Westward" *Little House*	*FACE
"Holland and Liberty" *Hans Brinker*	*FACE
"James Fenimore Cooper, First Novelist of the Republic"	
Deerslayer	*FACE
"New England Mind and Character" *Little Women*	*FACE
"Patriotic Women in the American Revolution" *Abigail Adams*	*FACE
"Robinson Crusoe Syllabus" *Robinson Crusoe*	*FACE
"Switzerland and Liberty" *Heidi*	*FACE
"William Penn and the Pennsylvania Colony of Religious	
Toleration" *Benjamin West*	*FACE
"We Three" *Spirit of St. Louis*	*FACE
"Teaching of Providential History:" Bradford's *Of Plimoth*	
Plantation and the Pilgrims	*FACE
Smith, Captain John	
Captain John Smith's America ed. by John Lankford	HARPER
Smith, Captain John, Biographies of:	
John Smith, Man of Adventure by Miriam E. Mason	HOUGHTON
Three Worlds of Captain John Smith by Philip L. Barbour	HOUGHTON
Smith, Nora Archibald	
Kate Douglas Wiggin, As Her Sister Knew Her (reprint)	WEST

	Order From, or Out-of-Print
Stevenson, Burton Egbert	
American History in Verse,	BOB JONES
Home Book of Verse for Young Folks, The	HOLD, RINEHART
Stevenson, Robert Louis	
Child's Garden of Verses, A, Illus. by Fujikawa	FACE
Treasure Island	FACE
Stevenson, Robert Louis, Biography of:	
Robert Louis Stevenson: Storyteller & Adventurer by Katharine Wilkie	HOUGHTON
Steinberg, Alfred	
Admiral Richard E. Byrd	PUTNAM
Stone, Irving	
Greek Treasure, Biog. Novel of Henry & Sophia Schliemann	BANTAM
Stuart, Jesse	
Thread That Runs So True: Story of a Kentucky Mountain School-Teacher	FACE
Thane, Elswyth	
Mount Vernon Family	MT. VERNON
Mount Vernon is Ours: Preservation…of Washington's Home	MT. VERNON
Potomac Squire	MT. VERNON
Washington's Lady: Life of Martha Washington	MT. VERNON
Trelease, Jim	
Read-Aloud Handbook	PENGUIN
Wallace, Lew	
Ben Hur: A Tale of the Christ	FACE
Ben Hur: A Tale of the Christ – Teacher's Guide	OP
Wallace, Lew, Biographies of:	
Lew Wallace: Boy Writer by Martha Schaaf	OP
Lew Wallace: Militant Romantic by Robert & Katherine Morseberger	MCGRAW-HILL
Watts, Isaac	
Divine Songs in Easy Language for the Use of Children	CUMBERLAND
Warren, Mercy	
History of the…American Revolution (see *Consider and Ponder,* FACE)	
The Group, a play, (see *Consider and Ponder,* FACE)	
Wayland, John W.	
Pathfinder of the Seas: Life of Matthew Fontaine Maury	OP
Webster, Noah	
American Dictionary of the English Language (1828)	FACE
Webster, Noah, Biographies of:	
Noah Webster: Father of the Dictionary by Isabel Proudfit	*OP
Noah Webster: Founding Father…, by Slater, *American Dictionary*	FACE
Wheatley, Phillis	
Poems of Phillis Wheatley ed. by Julian D. Macon, Jr.	U. OF NC
Wiggin, Kate Douglas	
Bird's Christmas Carol, The	OP
Mother Carey's Chickens	FACE
Rebecca of Sunnybrook Farm (Airmont)	FACE
Writings of Kate Douglas Wiggin: A Child's Journey with Dickens	OP
Wiggin, Kate Douglas, Biography of:	
Kate Douglas Wiggin as Her Sister Knew Her by Nora Archibald Smith (reprint)	WEST
Wilbur, General William H.	
Making of George Washington, Patriotic Ed.	FACE
Making of Geo. Washington: Family Study…Guide by Beth Ballenger	OP
Wilder, Laura Ingalls	
Farmer Boy	FACE
Little House in the Big Woods	*FACE
Wilder, Laura Ingalls, Biography of:	
Laura by Donald Zochert	HARPER
Wilkie, Katharine	
Robert Louis Stevenson: Storyteller & Adventurer	MACMILLAN
Williams, Frances Leigh	
Matthew Fontaine Maury: Scientist of the Sea	RUTGERS U.
Ocean Pathfinder: Biography of Matthew Fontaine Maury	HARCOURT
Williams, Margery	
The Velveteen Rabbit	BANTAM
Williams, Professor Stanley	
Biography of Washington Irving	OXFORD U.
Winslow, Edward	
Good News from Virginia	OP
Woodward, Grace Steele	
Pocahontas, U. of OK	FACE
Wyss, J. R.	
Swiss Family Robinson, The	PUTNAM
Yates, Elizabeth	
Amos Fortune, Free Man, Dutton	PENGUIN

PUBLISHERS' ADDRESS AND PHONE FOR ORDERING

To update the information below, check the current edition of *Books in Print* by R.R. Bowker through your local bookstore or library.

Airmont Publishing Co., Inc.
401 Lafayette St., NY, NY 10003; 1-800-223-5251

American Christian History Institute (ACHI)
P.O. Box 648, Palo Cedro, CA 96073;
916-547-3535

A M S Press, Inc.
56 E. 13th St., NY, NY 10003; 212-777-4700

Ayer Co. Publishers, Inc.
P.O. Box 958, Salem, NH 03079; 800-282-5413

Bantam Doubleday Dell
666 Fifth Ave., NY, NY 10103; 800-223-6834

Belknap Press (see **Harvard Univ. Press**)

Biblio Distribution Center
81 Adams Dr., Totowa, NJ 10103; 200-256-8600

Bob Jones University
Greenville, South Carolina 29614

Bobbs-Merrill Co., (see **Macmillan**)

Cumberland Missionary Society
c/o Carris Kocher, P.O. Box 912
Concordsville, PA 19331; 610-459-2093

Dodd, Mead & Company
6 Ram Ridge Rd., Spring Valley, NY 10977;
800-237-3255

Dutton, E. P. (see **Penguin**)

Everyman (see **Biblio Dist.**)

Foundation for American Christian Education (F.A.C.E.)
Box 9588, Chesapeake, VA 23321; 800-352-FACE

Garrard Publishing Co.
1607 N. Market St., Champaign, IL 61820;
217-521-6839

George F. Cram, Inc. (Maps)
301 S. LaSalle St., Indianapolis, IN 46206;
317-635-5564

Gordon Press Publishers
P.O. Box 459 Bowling Grn. Sta., NY, NY 10004

Grossett & Dunlap (see **Putnam**)

Harcourt Brace Jovanovich
1250 Sixth Ave., San Diego, CA 92101;
800-543-1918; 800-782-4479

Harper Collins (Harper & Row)
1000 Keystone Industrial Park, Scranton, PA 18512;
1-800-242-7737

Harvard University Press
79 Garden St., Cambridge, MA 02138;
617-495-2600

Haskell Booksellers, Inc.
P.O. Box 420, Blythebourne Station
Brooklyn, NY 11219; 718-435-7878

Henry Regnery, Co. (see **Regnery Gateway**)

Hold, Rinehart and Winston
6277 Sea Harbor Dr., Orlando, FL 32887;
800-782-4479

Houghton Mifflin Co.
925 East Meadow Dr., Palo Alto, CA 94303;
800-982-6111; 800-225-3362

Libros CLIE, c/o TSELF, Inc.
3585 NW 54th St., Ft.Lauderdale, FL 33309

Little, Brown & Company
34 Beacon, Boston, MA 02108; 800-343-9204

Long House, The
P.O. Box 3, New Canaan, CN 06840-2931;
203-966-2931

Macmillan Publishing Company
Front & Brown Sts., Riverside, NJ 08075;
800-257-5755

McGraw-Hill Book Company
Princeton Rd., Hightstown, NJ 08520;
800-722-4726

Mile-Hi Publishers
P.O. Box 40550, Mesa, AZ 85274;
800-369-7323

Morrow, William, & Co., Inc.
Wilmor Warehouse, 39 Plymouth St.
Fairfield, NJ 07006; 800-843-9389

Mott Media
1000 E. Huron, Milford, MI 48042;
800-521-4350

Mount Vernon Ladies Association
Mail Order Dept., Mount Vernon, VA 22121

National Geographic Society
P.O. Box 1640, Washington, D.C. 20013-9861;
800-638-4077

New American Library, (c/o Penguin USA)

Noah Webster Educational Foundation
510-447-5692

Oxford University Press
200 Madison Ave., NY, NY 10016;
1-800-451-7556

Patriotic Education, Inc.
435 North Lee St., Alexandria, VA 22314;
703-548-3350

Penguin USA
120 Woodbine St., Bergenfield, NJ 07621;
800-526-0275

Pilgrim Institute, The
52549 Gumwood Rd., Granger, IL 46530;
219-277-1789

Prentice-Hall, Inc.
200 Old Tappan Rd., Old Tappan, NJ 07675;
800-634-2863

Putnam Publishing Group, The
390 Murray Hill Parkway
East Rutherford, NJ 07073-2185;
800-631-8571

Rand McNally, (see **Macmillan**)

Random House, Inc.
400 Hahn Rd., Westminster, MD 21157;
800-733-3000

Regnery Gateway, Inc.
1130 17th St., N.W.
Washington, D.C. 20036; 800-526-7626

Rutgers University Press
R.U.P. Distribution Ctr., P.O. Box 4869
Baltimore, MD 21211; 301-338-6947

Scholastic, Inc.
2931 East McCarty St.
Jefferson City, MO 65102
800-325-6149

Scott, Foresman & Co.
1900 E. Lake Ave., Glenview, IL 60025

Scribner, Charles, Sons, (see **Macmillan**)

Signet Classics
(see **New American Library**)

Simon & Schuster
1230 Ave. of the Americas
NY, NY 10020;
800-223-2348; 800-223-2336

Sleepy Hollow Restorations
Tarrytown, NY 10591

Tyndale House Publishers
336 Gundersen Dr., P.O. Box 80
Wheaton, IL 60189; 800-323-9400

University of Nebraska Press
901 N. 17th St., Lincoln, NE 68588-0520;
402-472-3581

Univ. of North Carolina Press
P.O. Box 2288
Chapel Hill, NC 27515-2288;
919-996-3561

University of Oklahoma Press
1005 Asp Avenue, Norman, OK 73019;
800-627-7377

Vanguard Press
424 Madison Ave., NY, NY 10017;
212-753-3906

Viking Penguin, Inc.; Viking Press
(see **Penguin USA**)

Walker and Company
(Div. of **Walker Publishing Co.**)
720 Fifth Ave., NY, NY 10019;
212-265-3632

William Morrow & Co., Inc.,
(see **Morrow, William, & Co., Inc.**)

Zenger Publishing Co., Inc.
P.O. Box 42026, Wash, DC 20015;
301-881-1470